H4 0

TEACH YOURSE[

D1098954

# FRENCH
# VOCABULARY

## A COMPLETE LEARNING TOOL

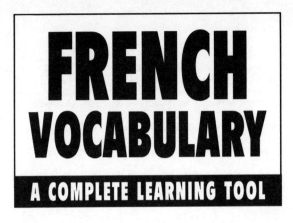

# FRENCH
# VOCABULARY
## A COMPLETE LEARNING TOOL

Series Editor: Rosi McNab

Language Editor: Nelly Moysan

**TEACH YOURSELF BOOKS**

For UK order queries: please contact Bookpoint Ltd, 130 Milton Park, Abingdon, Oxon OX14 4SB. Telephone: (44) 01235 400414, Fax: (44) 01235 400454. Lines are open from 9.00–6.00, Monday to Saturday, with a 24 hour message answering service. Email address: orders@bookpoint.co.uk

For U.S.A. & Canada order queries: please contact NTC/Contemporary Publishing, 4255 West Touhy Avenue, Lincolnwood, Illinois 60646 – 1975, U.S.A. Telephone: (847) 679 5500, Fax: (847) 679 2494.

Long-renowned as the authoritative source for self-guided learning – with more than 30 million copies sold worldwide – the *Teach Yourself* series includes over 200 titles in the fields of languages, crafts, hobbies, sports, and other leisure activities.

*British Library Cataloguing in Publication Data*
A catalogue record for this title is available from the British Library

*Library of Congress Catalog Card Number:* 95-71311

First published in UK 1996 by Hodder Headline Plc, 338 Euston Road, London NW1 3BH

First published in US 1996 by NTC/Contemporary Publishing, 4255 West Touhy Avenue, Lincolnwood (Chicago), Illinois 60646 – 1975 U.S.A.

Typeset by Transet Ltd, Coventry.
Printed in Great Britain for Hodder & Stoughton Educational, a division of Hodder Headline Plc, 338 Euston Road, London NW1 3BH by Cox & Wyman Ltd, Reading, Berkshire.

Impression number    13  12  11  10  9  8  7  6
Year                          2002  2001

# CONTENTS

# Contents

# INTRODUCTION

An easy-to-use reference book for key language for the language student, business traveller and holidaymaker.

## About this book

This book is designed to make learning easy. It can be used

- as a quick reference to find key words in a specific area
- to increase your word power by building up a stock of new vocabulary

## How to use the book

*Quick reference*
The topics are usually divided into sub-sections and the words in each topic are also in alphabetical order (in English) for easy reference. There is an example of how the words in each list might be used in a sentence.

*Vocabulary learning*
Follow the simple suggestions to help you to increase your vocabulary. There are also games and puzzles to make learning more fun.

## How can I learn better?

Most people complain of having a poor memory. They say they are no good at learning a language because they can't remember the words, but few people have difficulty in remembering things which really interest them: the names of members of a football team, the parts of a car, what happened in the last episode of a favourite radio or TV series, the ingredients in a recipe . . . !

## How can I make learning a list of words more interesting?

1 First YOU decide which list you are going to learn today.

**2** Then YOU decide which words in that list you want to try to learn.
Mark each word. (Put a mark beside each word you have chosen.)
Count them. (How many are you going to try to learn?)
Underline the first letter of each word. (What letters do they begin with?)

Now you are ready to begin.

**3** Say the words ALOUD. If you put your hands over your ears whilst
you read them it will cut out extraneous noise; this can help you to
concentrate by reflecting the sound of your voice, and to hear what
you sound like.

**4** Next look for ways to remember them. Do you know how YOU
remember words best? Try this quick test to find out:

Look at the grid for one minute, then cover it up and try to remember
as many words or pictures as possible.

Close the book and write down a list of the words you remember.

| horse | gate | banana | letter |
| bread | bottle | book | plane |
| shoe | scarf | knife | cup |

Have you remembered more words or more pictures?

**Words** If you have remembered more of the words than of the
pictures, you have a preference for memorising the written word and
you may find it helpful to write down the words you are learning.

**Pictures** If you have remembered more pictures, this shows you
have a more visual memory. You will probably find it helpful to 'tie in'
the words you learn to a picture.

You didn't remember many at all! Try again:

# Introduction

*Pictures*
Imagine a composite picture. Imagine a boat, 'put' the elephant, eating an apple, sitting on a chair in the boat. 'Put' the tap on the front of the boat to let the water out. (5 words.) Look through the window at a Christmas tree, 'hang' a mini-bicycle, the flower and the clock in the tree like Christmas decorations. Now put the light bulb on the top. What have you got left? The gloves. Put them on to keep your hands warm!

*Words*
There are four words which begin with b: ba...; boo...; bo... (you can eat two of them). There is one word for each of these initial sounds: c...; g...; h...; k...; l...; pl... Two words begin with s: sc...; sh... (and you can wear them both).

*Now how many can you remember?*
Which do you remember better, the words, the pictures or a bit of both? Try again in five minutes... and in half an hour... and tomorrow. Now you should know how you prefer to learn!

Below is a list of twelve words. Choose six of them to learn.

| | |
|---|---|
| *bridge* | **le pont** |
| *bus stop* | **l'arrêt de bus** |
| *car park* | **le parking** |
| *corner* | **le coin** |
| *crossroads* | **le carrefour** |
| *level crossing* | **le passage à niveau** |
| *one-way street* | **le sens unique** |
| *pedestrian area* | **la zone piétonne** |
| *road* | **la rue** |
| *station* | **la gare** |
| *traffic lights* | **les feux** |
| *tram* | **le tram** |

1 Put a **M**ark beside the words you would like to learn.
       **C**ount them. (Choose six to try.)
       **U**nderline the first letter of each word.

2 Read them aloud. (Put your hands over your ears whilst you do it.)

3 Try it again, until you are happy with the sound of them.

# *Introduction*

4 Look at each word carefully for ways to remember it. Find 'pegs' to hang them on.

*   Does it sound like the English word? (*parking*)
*   Does it sound like a different English word? (**pont** – sounds a bit like *pond*)
*   Does part of it look like the English word? (**arrêt de <u>bus</u>**)
*   Can you split it up into any bits you recognise? (**sens <u>unique</u>**)
*   Can you find any word that might be helpful? (**feux** – to do with *fire/light*)

\#   Can you see a picture of each word, as you say it?
\#   Can you picture it as it sounds?
    **pont** - *pond* picture a pond with a bridge over it.
    **coin** - *coin*  a coin has no corner, it's round!!!
    **feux** - *fur*  picture a furry animal, e.g. a cat, rubbing around a traffic light
\#   Can you build all the words into an imaginary composite picture?
    Say each word as you 'add' it to the picture e.g.
    **rue**, **pont**, **carrefour**, **route**, **parking**, **coin** etc . . .

5 Cover up the English and try to remember what your chosen words mean.

6 Write a list of the first letters and put dashes for the missing letters. Which did you choose? Mark them:

e.g. les feux – *traffic lights* (fire)
    le p_____ à n____ – *level crossing* (passage something)
    la g___ – *station* (begins like *garage*)
    le p___ – *bridge* (sounds like pond)
    l'a___ de b__ – *bus stop* (bus stopping place)
    le c___ – *corner* (same spelling as *coin*)
    le s___ u____ – *one-way street* (*way* unique)
    la z___ p_____ – *pedestrian area* (*zone* pedestrian)
    le c_____ – *crossroads* (carre: sounds like *car* – *four*: four roads)
    le p_____ – *car park* (parking. Pretty straightforward here!!)
    la r__ – *street* (same word exists – with a different meaning – in English language)
    le t___ – *tram* (tram-way)

and try to 'read' the words.

# Introduction

7 Fill in the missing letters and check that you have got them right.

8 Cover up the French and see if you can remember the words you have chosen.

9 Do something else for half an hour.

10 Go back and check that you can still remember the six you chose:

| e.g. *traffic lights* | les f__ |
| *level crossing* | le p_____ à n____ |
| *station* | la g___ |
| *bridge* | le p___ |
| *bus stop* | l'a___ de b__ |
| *corner* | le c___ |
| *one-way street* | le s__ u____ |
| *pedestrian area* | la z__ p_____ |
| *crossroads* | le c_____ |
| *car park* | le p_____ |
| *street* | la r__ |
| *tram* | le t___ |

## What do I know already?

Does it *sound* like the English word or a related word?
The German word for *chair* is **Stuhl** – it sounds like stool!
The Italian word for *town* is **città** – it sounds like city
The French word for *house* is **maison** – it sounds a bit like *mansion*
The Spanish word for *square* is **plaza** – it sounds a bit like *place*

Does it *look* like the English word or a related word?
The German word for *car* is **Wagen** – it looks a bit like *wagon*
The Italian word for *blue* is **azzuro** – it looks like *azure*
The French word for *red* is **rouge** – as rouge in make-up
The Spanish word for *garden* is **jardín** – it looks a bit like the English

Look for words that are similar to the English ones, for example:

**Journal** is a French word for *newspaper*. It looks like the English word *journal*. **Jour** means *day* in French so **journal** really means *a daily*. (You already know the expression **Bonjour** – *Good day*.) Now you have remembered two words – **jour** – *day*; **journal** – *newspaper*.

# *Introduction*

## Words that are related to words I already know

A brief look at some of the other European languages may help you to recognise patterns. This will help you to deduce the meaning of new words so that you can learn them more quickly:

|  | *German* | *French* | *Italian* | *related English word* |
|---|---|---|---|---|
| brother | Bruder | frère | fratello | fraternity |
| flower | Blumen | fleur | fiore | bloom/floral |
| foot | Fuß (Fuss) | pied | piede | pedal |
| grass | Gras | herbe | erba | herb |
| hunger | Hunger | faim | fame | famished |
| iron | Eisen | fer | ferro | ferrous (Fe) |
| man | Mann | homme | uomo | human |
| meat | Fleisch | viande | carne | carnivorous/flesh |
| water | Wasser | eau | acqua | aquarium |

English is a particularly rich language with words from many sources. Some of the words we use come from a northern origin, from the ancient Anglo-Saxon and Nordic languages, and some from a southern origin, from Latin, French and the Celtic languages, as well as many words brought back by the early travellers from all round the globe. For example *foot* is from the Teutonic or northern languages and *pedal* is from the Romance or southern languages. *Brother* is more like the German word **Bruder** but you can see the connection with the Italian **fratello** in words like *fraternity (brotherhood)*.

See if you can find English words which relate to these words:

|  | *French* | *Italian* | *related English word* |
|---|---|---|---|
| body | corps | corpo | |
| dress | robe | abito | |
| earth | terre | tierra | |
| horse | cheval | cavallo | |
| moon | lune | luna | |
| night | nuit | notte | |
| room | chambre | camera | |
| sea | mer | mare | |
| tooth | dent | dente | |
| wall | mur | muro | |

# *Introduction*

(cavalry chamber corporation corpse dentist habit lunar marine mermaid mural nocturnal robe vest terrestrial)

Can you find any more related words?

## Short cuts: looking for patterns

*Consonant changes*
Most consonants sound the same as in English. However, they are pronounced with a sharper sound. Here are the main exceptions:

c    pronounced as in English except for **ci** which is pronounced **si** in French (spécial)
ç    sounds like the **s** in *some* (garçon)
ch   sounds like **sh** in *shop* (château)
gn   sounds like **n** in *onion* (gagne)
h    is usually not pronounced at all (Hollande, Henri, homme)
j    sounds like **s** in *treasure* (je, toujours, Dijon)
qu   sounds like **k** (qui, quiche)
r    comes from the back of the throat (merci, très, trou)
t    usually similar to the English, but **t** is pronounced **s** in **-tion** (nation, élévation)
th   sounds like **t** (thème, Thomas)

*Final consonants*
If the last letter of a word is a consonant, it is usually not pronounced, except for:
**-l** – bal, mal, moral, carnaval
**-f** – œuf, bœuf
**-c** – cognac, sac, mec

*Vowels*
Most French vowels are found in English, but they do not always sound the same and are most of the time represented by different letters.

a    sounds like **a** in c**a**t (Paris, chocolat, banane)
e    sounds like **ea** in **ear**th (ne, je, de)
     (Note that it is pronounced faintly, if at all, at the end of a word.)
é    sounds similar to **ei** in **ei**ght (école, café)
è    sounds like **a** in b**a**re (père, mère, bière)
i    sounds like **ee** in b**ee**t (pire, Nice, Paris)
o    sounds like **o** in **o**dd (comme, olive, école)

# *Introduction*

u    a difficult sound for most English people, as it is not found in the English language. Put your lips in the right position, as if you were going to whistle. Now, without moving your lips, try to make the sound **ee** (sur, mur, dur)

Some sounds are the result of a combination of two or three vowels:

au, eau  sounds like **o** in *corporal* (eau, bateau, auto)
ou         sounds like **oo** in *pool* (moule, boule, croule)
ai          sounds like **e** above (*aigu, mai*)
oi          sounds like **wa**, as in in **o**ne (bois, moi, toiture)
eu         sounds like **u** in *sp**u**r* (beurre, coiffeur, deux)

*Nasal sounds*
These have no equivalent in English. All you have to do is listen very carefully to your French cassettes or radio stations and try to copy them.

an/en/am/em  France, pendant, vend, amant, allemand, dent, anglais
in/im/un/um  vin, impossible, un, humble
ain/ein        pain, peintre

## Word building

A lot of French words are just the same as in English, so you have fewer to learn: e.g. parking, week-end, bus, orange, cinéma, théâtre.

## Accents

We have already seen most of the accents in the paragraph related to vowel sounds. But there are a few more things you must remember!

– You do not generally put an accent on a capital letter (Episode; un épisode). (Many French textbooks add these accents to help you learn the spelling and pronunciation).
– When two vowels come together, and one has a tréma (¨) above it, each vowel is pronounced separately (Noël).
– An accent on a vowel (apart from e) indicates a different meaning (elle a; à Londres), (là; la), (sur; sûr), (ou; où).

## Liaisons

The final consonant of a word is often sounded if the word following

# *Introduction*

it starts with a vowel or a mute h, and its sound is carried over, particularly with **s** and **t**: nous⁀avons, il est⁀appétissant, vous êtes⁀Américains.

(Note that; when carried over in this way, **s** and **x** are pronounced like **z**, **d** like **t**, and **f** like **v**. **Et** is never run on, (but **est** is).

## Tips

**1** To learn the meaning of words with initial **é**, replace **é** with **s**: épice – *spice*, école – *school*, épouse – *spouse*, éponge – *sponge*.

**2** For -er verbs, final **é** is like final **-ed** in English (j'ai dansé – *I danced*; j'ai cuisiné – *I cooked*).

Most people make the excuse that they are no good at learning words as they have a poor memory. It isn't true. There is nothing wrong with your memory, but it often lacks the guidance and focus it needs. In learning words from a list the learner has not yet decided when he or she is going to use them. There is no immediate goal.

To learn with least effort you must choose your goals:

**A** I want to use the language to communicate with other speakers of that language:

  (*i*)   on a business trip
  (*ii*)  on a holiday trip
  (*iii*) on a social visit
  (*iv*)  at home, for business reasons
  (*v*)   because I know someone I would like to talk to or write to

**B** I want to be able to understand the language to:

  (*i*)   read something in that language for pleasure – books, magazines, letters, etc.
  (*ii*)  read something for business – manuals, letters, faxes, etc.
  (*iii*) listen to the radio
  (*iv*)  watch television programmes
  (*v*)   read signs and instructions on a visit

**C** I just enjoy learning languages.

You should choose the words and phrases you are going to learn and focus on them and their meaning. Concentrating on the words and

# *Introduction*

thinking about their meaning and the sound of them and looking for 'pegs' on which to hang them (looking for related words, imaging them in pictures, remembering the sound of the words, etc.) will help you to put them in your long-term memory.

How many of the picture words can you still remember... and how many of the written words?

Note: Abbreviations used throughout this book are (m.) for masculine, (f.) for feminine, (pl.) for plural.

# Les salutations *Greetings*

## FORMULES DE POLITESSE ET TITRES
### *GREETINGS AND TITLES*

| | | | |
|---|---|---|---|
| Bonjour | *Good morning* | Bonjour | *Hello* |
| Bonjour | *Good day* | Au revoir | *Goodbye* |
| Bonjour | *Good afternoon* | Salut | *Hi!* |
| Bonsoir | *Good evening* | À tout à l'heure | *See you later* |
| Bonne nuit | *Goodnight* | | |

---

## *ENCORE!*

● *Activity 1: What would you say?*

---

## Les titres *Titles*

| | | | |
|---|---|---|---|
| | | Monsieur | *Sir* |
| Monsieur | *Mr* | Docteur | *Doctor (medical)* |
| Mademoiselle | *Miss* | Docteur | *Doctor (title)* |
| Madame | *Mrs* | Professeur | *Professor (title)* |

---

## *ENCORE!*

● *Activity 2: What would you say?   Good morning:* Bonjour…

(a)   (b)   (c)

# Les nombres *Numbers*

## Les nombres cardinaux
### *Cardinal numbers*

| | |
|---|---|
| 0 | zéro |
| 1 | un |
| 2 | deux |
| 3 | trois |
| 4 | quatre |
| 5 | cinq |
| 6 | six |
| 7 | sept |
| 8 | huit |
| 9 | neuf |
| 10 | dix |
| 11 | onze |
| 12 | douze |
| 13 | treize |
| 14 | quatorze |
| 15 | quinze |
| 16 | seize |
| 17 | dix-sept |
| 18 | dix-huit |
| 19 | dix-neuf |
| 20 | vingt |
| 21 | vingt et un |
| 22 | vingt-deux |
| 23 | vingt-trois |
| 24 | vingt-quatre |
| 25 | vingt-cinq |
| 26 | vingt-six |
| 27 | vingt-sept |
| 28 | vingt-huit |
| 29 | vingt-neuf |
| 30 | trente |
| 31 | trente et un |
| 40 | quarante |
| 41 | quarante et un |
| 50 | cinquante |
| 60 | soixante |
| 70 | soixante-dix |
| 71 | soixante et onze |
| 72 | soixante-douze |
| 75 | soixante-quinze |
| 80 | quatre-vingts |
| 81 | quatre-vingt-un |
| 89 | quatre-vingt-neuf |
| 90 | quatre-vingt-dix |
| 91 | quatre-vingt-onze |
| 95 | quatre-vingt-quinze |
| 99 | quatre-vingt-dix-neuf |
| 100 | cent |
| 101 | cent un |
| 200 | deux cents |
| 201 | deux cent un |
| 1000 | mille |
| 1999 | mille neuf cent quatre-vingt-dix-neuf |
| *or* | dix-neuf cent quatre-vingt-dix-neuf |

## Les nombres ordinaux
### *Ordinal numbers*

| | |
|---|---|
| le premier / la première | *first* |
| le second / la seconde / le deuxième | *second* |
| le troisième | *third* |
| le quatrième | *fourth* |
| le cinquième | *fifth* |
| le dixième | *tenth* |
| le vingtième | *twentieth* |
| le vingt et unième | *twenty-first* |
| le n-ième | *nth; umpteenth* |
| une fois | *once* |
| deux fois | *twice* |
| trois fois | *three times* |
| le quart | *quarter* |
| la moitié | *half* |

# Les nombres *Numbers*

## ENCORE!

● *Activity 1: Practise reading these telephone numbers and codes.*

The code for France from the UK is 00 33 (zéro zéro trente-trois). For Paris use 00 33 1 (zéro zéro, trente-trois, un).

Say the numbers in pairs, for example (00 33) 25 42 50 19 – zéro zéro, trente-trois, vingt-cinq, quarante-deux, cinquante, dix-neuf.

Try these:   (00 33) 30 97 78 36
                (00 33) 52 23 86 40
                (00 33 1) 49 65 26 21
                (00 33 1) 80 27 13 95

● *Activity 2: (a) Read these years aloud:*

1975 _____ 1984 _____
1998 _____ 2025 _____

(b) Add important dates in your own life and practise saying them:

    *I was born in …* **Je suis né(e) en** _____

● *Activity 3: The Big Race: Where did they come?*

Marie            Virginie           Paulette

13

# Le calendrier *The calendar*

| | |
|---|---|
| un jour | *day* |
| une semaine | *week* |
| un mois | *month* |
| une année | *year* |
| une année bissextile | *Leap year* |

## Les jours de la semaine
### *Days of the week*

| | |
|---|---|
| lundi | *Monday* |
| mardi | *Tuesday* |
| mercredi | *Wednesday* |
| jeudi | *Thursday* |
| vendredi | *Friday* |
| samedi | *Saturday* |
| dimanche | *Sunday* |
| le matin | *morning* |
| le midi | *midday* |
| l'après-midi (m.) | *afternoon* |
| le soir | *evening* |
| la nuit | *night* |
| aujourd'hui | *today* |
| demain | *tomorrow* |
| après-demain | *the day after tomorrow* |
| hier | *yesterday* |
| avant-hier | *the day before yesterday* |
| ce matin | *this morning* |
| hier après-midi | *yesterday afternoon* |
| demain soir | *tomorrow evening* |
| le weekend | *the weekend* |

## Les mois *Months*

| | |
|---|---|
| janvier | *January* |
| février | *February* |
| mars | *March* |
| avril | *April* |
| mai | *May* |
| juin | *June* |
| juillet | *July* |
| août | *August* |
| septembre | *September* |
| octobre | *October* |
| novembre | *November* |
| décembre | *December* |

## Les dates *Dates*

Cardinal numbers (deux, trois, quatre, etc.) are used for dates, except for the first of each month (le premier).

| | |
|---|---|
| le premier janvier | *1st January* |
| le deux février | *2nd February* |
| le trois mars | *3rd March* |
| le vingt avril | *20th April* |
| le vingt et un mai | *21st May* |

## Les quatre saisons
### *The four seasons*

| | |
|---|---|
| (en) hiver | *(in) winter* |
| (au) printemps | *(in) spring* |
| (en) été | *(in) summer* |
| (en) automne | *(in) autumn* |

## Les fêtes
### *Holidays and celebrations*

| | |
|---|---|
| Noël | *Christmas* |
| la veille de Noël | *Christmas Eve* |
| le nouvel an | *New Year* |
| la Saint-Sylvestre | *New Year's Eve* |
| le jour de l'an | *New Year's Day* |
| la chandeleur | *Candlemas* |
| le Mardi gras | *Shrove Tuesday* |
| Pâques | *Easter* |
| le Vendredi saint | *Good Friday* |

# Le calendrier *The calendar*

| la fête nationale | *Bastille day* | | Bonne Année! | *Happy New Year!* |
|---|---|---|---|---|
| la Toussaint | *All Saints' Day* | | Joyeuses | |
| Joyeux Noël! | *Happy Christmas!* | | Pâques! | *Happy Easter!* |

---

## *ENCORE!*

● *Activity:*

(a) C'est quand, ton/votre anniversaire? *When is your birthday?*
Mon anniversaire est le \_\_\_\_\_ *My birthday is* \_\_\_\_\_

Say when the birthdays are of all the members of your family.

(b) You have meetings on these days. Say them in French.

# L'heure *The time*

## QUELLE HEURE EST-IL?
### *WHAT TIME IS IT?*

| | | | |
|---|---|---|---|
| Il est une heure | *It is one o'clock* | une heure et demie | *half past one* |
| une heure cinq | *five past one* | deux heures moins le quart | *quarter to two* |
| une heure dix | *ten past one* | deux heures moins dix | *ten to two* |
| une heure et quart | *quarter past one* | deux heures | *two o'clock* |
| une heure vingt | *twenty past one* | | |

| | |
|---|---|
| 13.07 | treize heures sept |
| 15.19 | quinze heures dix-neuf |
| 19.54 | dix-neuf heures cinquante-quatre |
| 22.47 | vingt-deux heures quarante-sept |

| | |
|---|---|
| midi | *midday* |
| minuit | *midnight* |
| Votre montre avance/retarde. | *Your watch is fast / slow.* |
| Désolé(e) d'être en retard. | *Sorry I'm late.* |
| Ma montre ne marche pas/ est cassée. | *My watch doesn't work / is broken.* |
| J'ai perdu ma montre. | *I have lost my watch.* |
| Il me faut une nouvelle pile pour ma montre. | *I need a new battery for my watch.* |

## ENCORE!

● *Activity: When shall we meet? Practise saying these times.*

Let's meet at…                On se retrouve à …

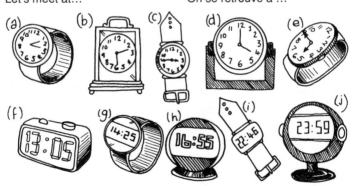

16

# Les couleurs *Colours*

| | | | |
|---|---|---|---|
| beige | *beige* | rouge | *red* |
| noir(e) | *black* | argenté(e) | *silver* |
| bleu(e) | *blue* | turquoise | *turquoise* |
| brun(e) | *brown* | blanc(he) | *white* |
| *marron | *brown* | jaune | *yellow* |
| doré(e) | *gold* | foncé(e) | *dark* |
| vert(e) | *green* | clair(e)/pâle | *light / pale* |
| gris(e) | *grey* | vif/vive | *bright* |
| naturel(le) | *natural* | fluorescent(e) | *fluorescent* |
| bleu-marine | *navy* | | |
| *orange | *orange* | *marron *and* orange *never change* | |
| rose | *pink* | *for feminine or plural* (des rideaux | |
| violet(te) | *purple* | orange, des chaussures marron) | |

## *ENCORE!*

● *Activity 1: What colours would you like them to be? Describe the jerseys and trousers:*

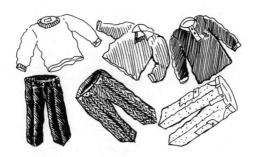

● *Activity 2: What colours are the flags?*

| UK | Italy | France | Germany | Spain |
|---|---|---|---|---|

# C'est comment? *What is it like?*

## LES ADJECTIFS
### *ADJECTIVES*

You can use these adjectives to say something about, or describe, things, people, places, or feelings. You will also find appropriate adjectives included in the topic areas.

| | |
|---|---|
| actif (-ive) | *active* |
| vivant(e) | *alive* |
| vieux/vieille | *ancient* |
| affreux (-euse) | *awful* |
| mauvais(e) | *bad* |
| beau/belle | *beautiful* |
| grand(e) }<br>gros/grosse } | *big* |
| amer (-ère) | *bitter* |
| aveugle | *blind* |
| brusque | *blunt, brusque* |
| ennuyeux (-euse) | *boring* |
| courageux (-euse) | *brave* |
| brillant(e) | *bright* |
| large | *broad* |
| occupé(e) | *busy* |
| bon marché | *cheap* |
| propre | *clean* |
| intelligent(e) | *clever* |
| fermé(e) | *closed* |
| froid(e) | *cold* |
| ordinaire | *common* |
| compliqué(e) | *complicated* |
| frais/fraîche | *cool* |
| lâche | *cowardly* |
| sombre | *dark* |
| mort(e) | *dead* |
| sourd(e) | *deaf* |
| cher (-ère) | *dear; expensive* |
| chéri(e) | *dear; beloved* |
| profond(e) | *deep* |
| sale | *dirty* |
| double | *double* |
| affreux (-euse) | *dreadful* |
| sec/sèche | *dry* |
| terne | *dull* |
| tôt | *early* |
| facile | *easy* |
| vide | *empty* |
| occupé(e) | *engaged* (occupied) |
| clair(e) | *fair* |
| faux/fausse | *false* |
| célèbre | *famous* |
| loin | *far* |
| rapide | *fast* |
| gros/grosse | *fat, large* |
| premier (-ière) | *first* |
| en forme | *fit* |
| plat(e) | *flat* |
| fragile | *fragile* |
| frais/fraîche | *fresh* |
| gratuit(e) | *free* (no cost) |
| disponible | *free* (available) |
| plein(e) | *full* |
| drôle | *funny* |
| généreux (-euse) | *generous* |
| bon(ne) | *good* |
| beau/belle | *good-looking* |
| coupable | *guilty* |
| handicappé(e) | *handicapped* |
| beau/belle | *handsome* |
| heureux (-euse) | *happy* |
| dur(e) | *hard* |
| lourd(e) | *heavy* |
| haut(e) | *high* |
| horrible | *horrible* |
| chaud(e) | *hot* |
| oisif (-ive) | *idle* |
| malade | *ill* |
| impossible | *impossible* |
| innocent(e) | *innocent* |
| intelligent(e) | *intelligent* |
| intéressant(e) | *interesting* |
| gentil(le) | *kind* |
| boiteux (-euse) | *lame* |
| dernier (-ière) | *last* |
| tard | *late* |

# C'est comment? *What is it like?*

| | | | | |
|---|---|---|---|---|
| paresseux (-euse) | *lazy* | | pointu(e) | *sharp* |
| gauche | *left* | | court(e) | *short* |
| clair(e) | *light* | | simple | *simple* |
| vivant(e) | *lively* | | unique | *single* |
| long(ue) | *long* | | lent(e) | *slow* |
| fort(e)/bruyant(e) | *loud* | | petit(e) | *small* |
| bas/basse | *low* | | lisse | *smooth* |
| radin(e) | *mean* | | doux/douce | *soft* |
| moderne | *modern* | | rance | *stale* |
| étroit(e) | *narrow* | | fort(e) | *strong* |
| méchant(e) | *nasty* | | stupide | *stupid* |
| près | *near* | | sucré(e) | *sweet* |
| nouveau/ | | | apprivoisé(e) | *tame* |
| nouvelle | *new* | | tendre | *tender* |
| gentil(le) | *nice* | | mince | *thin* |
| vieux/vieille | *old* | | fatigué(e) | *tired* |
| ouvert(e) | *open* | | robuste | *tough* |
| passif (-ive) | *passive* | | vrai(e) | *true* |
| poli(e) | *polite* | | laid(e) | *ugly* |
| possible | *possible* | | inapte | *unfit* |
| joli(e) | *pretty* | | méchant(e) | *unkind* |
| tranquille | *quiet* | | chaud(e) | *warm* |
| rare | *rare* | | faible | *weak* |
| réel(le) | *real* | | bien | *well* |
| droit(e) | *right* | | mouillé(e) | *wet* |
| brutal(e) | *rough* | | large | *wide* |
| impoli(e) | *rude* | | sauvage | *wild* |
| triste | *sad* | | faux/fausse | *wrong* |
| peu profond(e) | *shallow* | | jeune | *young* |

## ENCORE!

● *Activity: Choose any twelve words from the list. Write them down and then write their opposites beside them.*

| bon | mauvais | chaud | _____ |
|---|---|---|---|
| _____ | _____ | _____ | _____ |
| _____ | _____ | _____ | _____ |
| _____ | _____ | _____ | _____ |
| _____ | _____ | _____ | _____ |
| _____ | _____ | _____ | _____ |

# C'est comment? *What is it like?*

## LES ADVERBS *ADVERBS*

You can use these adverbs to modify what you are saying about something,

e.g.
Elle est **assez** grande.              *She is **quite** tall.*
Il est **toujours** en retard.          *He is **always** late.*

| | | | |
|---|---|---|---|
| presque | *almost* | seulement | *only* |
| aussi | *also* | peut-être | *perhaps* |
| au moins | *at least* | probablement | *probably* |
| en moyenne | *on average* | assez | *quite* |
| complètement | *completely* | plutôt | *rather* |
| assez | *enough* | réellement | *really* |
| même | *even* | particulièrement | *specially* |
| en fait | *indeed* | malheureusement | |
| moins | *less* | | *unfortunately* |
| plus | *more* | très | *very* |

---

## ENCORE!

● *Activity: Modify these sentences by adding a word.*

Elle est _____ grande. Je suis _____ fatiguée.
Ils sont _____ en retard.

_____ M. Lebrun ne peut pas vous recevoir aujourd'hui.
_____ pourriez-vous venir demain.

---

# C'est où? *Where is it?*

## OÙ?
### WHERE?

| | |
|---|---|
| au-dessus de | *above* |
| autour de | *around* |
| à la (f.), au (m.) | *at the* |
| chez | *at* (someone's house) |
| derrière | *behind* |
| près de | *beside* |
| sous | *below, under* |
| entre | *between* |
| par delà | *beyond* |
| en bas | *down, below* |
| partout | *everywhere* |
| loin de | *far from* |
| en avant | *forward* |
| ici | *here* |
| à la maison | *(at) home* |
| dans | *in* |
| devant | *in front of* |
| à l'intérieur de | *inside* |
| près de | *near to* |
| nulle part | *nowhere* |
| sur | *on* |
| en face de | *opposite* |
| à l'extérieur de | *outside* |
| de l'autre côté de | *on the other side of / over* |
| par dessus | *on top of / over* |
| après | *past* |
| quelque part | *somewhere* |
| là | *there* |
| à travers | *through* |
| à | *to* |
| sous | *under* |
| en haut | *up* |
| sur | *on top of* |

## ENCORE!

● Activity: Where is he?

21

# C'est quand? *When is it?*

## ENCORE!

● *Activity: Add a word to complete these sentences.*

Nous allons _____ en France en vacances.
Nous allons _____ en ville.
_____ nous sommes allés à Paris.
_____ il fait beau mais il pleut _____ .

## LES PETITS MOTS D'INTERROGATION
### *QUESTION WORDS*

| | |
|---|---|
| Comment? | *How?* |
| Combien de? | *How many?* |
| Combien? | *How much?* |
| | |
| Quelle sorte de ...? | *What kind of ...?* |
| Quoi? | *What?* |
| | |
| Comment? | *What? (Pardon?)* |
| Qu'est-ce que tu veux? | *What do you want?* |
| Qu'est-ce que tu mets? | *What are you wearing?* |
| Qu'est-ce que tu fais? | *What are you doing?* |
| | |
| Quand? | *When?* |
| C'est quand la boum? | *When is the party?* |
| | |
| Où? | *Where?* |
| On se retrouve où? | *Where shall we meet?* |
| | |
| Quel(le)/Lequel? | *Which?* |
| Quelle est la route pour aller à ...? | *Which way is it to ...?* |
| Lequel tu aimes? | *Which one do you like?* |
| | |
| Qui? | *Who?* |
| Qui y va? | *Who is going?* |
| | |
| Pourquoi? | *Why?* |
| Pourquoi tu es en retard? | *Why are you late?* |
| | |
| Comment? | *How?* |
| Comment allez-vous? | *How are you?* |

# Les questions *Questions*

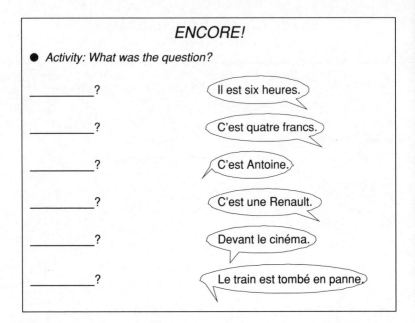

ENCORE!

● *Activity: What was the question?*

_____?        Il est six heures.

_____?        C'est quatre francs.

_____?        C'est Antoine.

_____?        C'est une Renault.

_____?        Devant le cinéma.

_____?        Le train est tombé en panne.

# Les articles et les pronoms *Articles and pronouns*

## le/la/l'/les  *the*

Use **le** with masculine words: **le** château, **le** train, **le** gâteau.
   **la** with feminine words: **la** maison, **la** voiture, **la** pomme.
   **l'** with masculine or feminine words beginning with a vowel or **h**:
   **l'**église, **l'**ami, **l'**homme, **l'**heure.

*Note*: In some words **h** acts like a consonant even though it is silent:
**le** haricot, **le** hibou.

Use **les** with all plural words: **les** enfants, **les** garçons, **les** filles.

## un/une  *a*

Use **un** with masculine words: **un** château, **un** train, **un** gâteau.
   **une** with feminine words: **une** maison, **une** voiture, **une** pomme.

## du/de la/de l'/des  *some, any*

Use **des** with all plural words: **des** trains, **des** voitures, **des** enfants.
   **du** with masculine words: **du** café, **du** fromage, **du** pain.
   **de la** with feminine words: **de la** viande, **de la** crème, **de la** tarte.
   **de l'** with masculine or feminine words beginning with a vowel or **h**:
   **de l'**énergie, **de l'**eau, **de l'**huile.

Use **du/de la/de l'/des** to mean *any* in a question: Vous avez **du** beurre?
(*Have you got any butter?*), Tu as **des** sœurs? (*Have you any sisters?*), Tu
as **de la** monnaie? (*Have you got any change?*).

## chaque, tous/toutes  *every*

Use **chaque** with a singular noun or **tous/toutes** with a plural noun:
Il se leve **chaque** jour à 7h. (*He gets up at 7 o'clock every day.*)
Il se leve **tous** les jours à 7h.

Nous regardons cette émission **chaque** semaine./Nous regardons cette
émission **toutes** les semaines. (*We watch this programme every week.*)

# Les articles et les pronoms *Articles and pronouns*

## ce/cet/cette/ces *this/that, these/those*

Use **ce** with masculine nouns: **ce** vin, **ce** sandwich.
   **cette** with feminine nouns: **cette** bière, **cette** femme.
   **cet** with masculine singular words beginning with a vowel or **h**:
      **cet** animal, **cet** homme.
   **ces** with all plural nouns: **ces** vins, **ces** femmes, **ces** hommes.

To show the difference between *this* and *that*, add **-ci** or **-là** to the noun:
   **Ce** vin-**ci** est sec; **ce** vin-**là** est doux.

## celui/celle/ceux/celles *this/that one, these/those ones*

Use these words to refer to something already mentioned.

Add **-ci** or **-là** to show the difference between *this one* or *that one*:
Quel est ton manteau? **Celui-là.** (*Which is your coat? That one.*)
Je cherche des bottes. **Celles-ci** sont pratiques. (*I'm looking for some boots. These ones are sturdy.*)

## y *there*

Use **y** instead of repeating a place:   Tu travailles à Paris? Oui, **j'y** travaille.
                                          Il va à la campagne? Non, il **n'y** va pas.

## en *some*

Use **en** instead of repeating du/de la/de l'/des and a noun:
   Vous avez des enfants? **J'en** ai trois.
   Tu veux du café? Merci. Je n'**en** veux pas.

# Les articles et les pronoms *Articles and pronouns*

## *PERSONAL PRONOUNS*

| | | | |
|---|---|---|---|
| **je** | je travaille | *I work* | (subject pronoun) |
| **moi** | c'est moi! | *it's me!* | (emphatic pronoun) |
| **me** | Sylvie me regarde | *Sylvie is watching me* | (direct object pronoun) |
| **me** | André me parle | *André is speaking to me* | (indirect object pronoun) |
| **tu** | tu travailles | *you work* | |
| **toi** | c'est toi! | *it's you!* | |
| **te** | Sylvie te regarde | *Sylvie is watching you* | |
| **te** | André te parle | *André is speaking to you* | |
| **il** | il travaille | *he works* | |
| **lui** | c'est lui! | *it's him!* | |
| **le** | Sylvie le regarde | *Sylvie is watching him* | |
| **lui** | André lui parle | *André is speaking to him* | |
| **elle** | elle travaille | *she works* | |
| **elle** | c'est elle! | *it's her!* | |
| **la** | Sylvie la regarde | *Sylvie is watching her* | |
| **lui** | André lui parle | *André is speaking to her* | |
| **nous** | nous travaillons | *we work* | |
| **nous** | c'est nous! | *it's us!* | |
| **nous** | Sylvie nous regarde | *Sylvie is watching us* | |
| **nous** | André nous parle | *André is speaking to us* | |
| **vous** | vous travaillez | *you work* | |
| **vous** | c'est vous! | *it's you!* | |
| **vous** | Sylvie vous regarde | *Sylvie is watching you* | |
| **vous** | André vous parle | *André is speaking to you* | |
| **ils** | ils travaillent | *they work* (m.pl.) | |
| **eux** | c'est eux! | *it's them!* | |
| **les** | Sylvie les regarde | *Sylvie is watching them* | |
| **leur** | André leur parle | *André is speaking to them* | |
| **elles** | elles travaillent | *they work* (f.pl.) | |
| **elles** | c'est elles! | *it's them!* | |
| **les** | Sylvie les regarde | *Sylvie is watching them* | |
| **leur** | André leur parle | *André is speaking to them* | |

# Les pronoms et les conjonctions *Pronouns and conjunctions*

## POSSESSIVE ADJECTIVES AND PRONOUNS

| | | | | |
|---|---|---|---|---|
| *my* | mon | ma | mes | mes |
| *mine* | le mien | la mienne | les miens | les miennes |
| *your* | ton | ta | tes | tes |
| *yours* | le tien | la tienne | les tiens | les tiennes |
| *his / her* | son | sa | ses | ses |
| *his / hers* | le sien | la sienne | les siens | les siennes |
| *our* | notre | notre | nos | nos |
| *ours* | le nôtre | la nôtre | les nôtres | les nôtres |
| *your* | votre | votre | vos | vos |
| *yours* | le vôtre | la vôtre | les vôtres | les vôtres |
| *their* | leur | leur | leurs | leurs |
| *theirs* | le leur | la leur | les leurs | les leurs |

These agree with the word they describe, not with the owner, for example:

Elle a perdu **son** sac.      *She has lost her bag.*

Il a oublié **ses** gants.      *He has forgotten his gloves.*

## CONJUNCTIONS

| | | | |
|---|---|---|---|
| et | *and* | parce que | *because* |
| mais | *but* | ou | *or* |
| bien que | *although* | si | *if* |
| pourtant | *however* | néanmoins | *nevertheless* |
| pendant que | *whilst* | puisque | *since, as* |
| peut-être | *perhaps* | malgré | *in spite of* |

# **Verbes** *Verbs*

## *VERBS*

There are three main categories of French verbs, according to the ending of the infinitive: -**er**, -**re**, -**ir** (e.g. par**ler** – to speak, vend**re** – to sell, fin**ir** – to finish). Some verbs are regular, which means that they follow a particular pattern. Others are irregular, as they deviate from this pattern in places.

The main verb tenses are: the present, the perfect, the imperfect and the future. (For more information on verbs, see *Teach Yourself French Verbs*.)

## *The present*

The present tense describes ● a regular event or activity
                                                 ● what is happening now

e.g. Je parle français. *I speak French.*
　　Je parle au téléphone en ce moment. *I am speaking on the phone at the moment.*

Some of the most used French verbs (avoir – *to have*, être – *to be*, aller – *to go* and faire – *to do*) are irregular. For their forms in the present tense, see page 31.

**-er verbs**
About 80 percent of French verbs are regular -**er** verbs. Although there are some slight variations they nearly all follow this pattern.

| Parler *to speak* | je parle | nous parlons |
| | tu parles | vous parlez |
| | il/elle/on parle | ils/elles parlent |

**-re verbs**

| Vendre *to sell* | je vends | nous vendons |
| | tu vends | vous vendez |
| | il/elle/on vend | ils/elles vendent |

**-ir verbs**

| finir *to finish* | je finis | nous finissons |
| | tu finis | vous finissez |
| | il/elle/on finit | ils/elles finissent |

## *The perfect*

The perfect tense describes an action completed in the past.
It is made up of the present tense of **avoir** or **être** + past participle
e.g.  j'**ai** mangé   *I ate*                     je **suis** tombé   *I fell*
                      *I have eaten*                            *I have fallen*

The past participles of regular verbs are formed by removing -**er**, -**re** or -**ir**
from the infinitive and adding -**e**, -**u** or -**i** (j'ai parl**é**, j'ai vend**u**, j'ai fin**i**).
But the past participles of irregular verbs do not follow a pattern: avoir – eu,
être – été, faire – fait, prendre – pris, boire – bu.

Most verbs use **avoir** to make the perfect
e.g. j'**ai** parlé *I spoke*, tu **as** oublié *you have forgotten*, nous **avons** attendu
*we waited*, ils **ont** choisi *they have chosen*.

Only a few verbs use **être** to make the perfect. They are verbs expressing
movement or a change of state: aller, venir, arriver, entrer, rentrer, partir,
sortir, descendre, monter, tomber, rester, devenir, naitre, mourir.

The past participles of these verbs agree with their subject. So we must add
**e** to the past particple if the subject is feminine, **s** if it is plural and **es** if it is
both feminine and plural e.g. je suis entré**e** *I*(f.) *went in*, elle est arrivé**e**, *she
has arrived*, ils sont venu**s** *they came*, elles sont parti**es** *they've* (f.pl.) *left*.

Reflexive verbs also use **être** to form the perfect, for example:
    Je me suis levé(e) à 8h.   *I got up at 8.*

## *The imperfect*

The imperfect tense expresses  ● something that used to happen in the past
                               ● how things were in the past
                               ● what was happening (imperfect) when
                                 something else occurred (perfect).

It is formed by removing the -**ons** ending from the nous form of the present
and replacing it with -**ais**, -**ais**, -**ait**, -**ions**, -**iez**, -**aient**, for example:

    J'allais au cinéma toutes les semaines.   *I used to go to the cinema
      every week.*
    Notre maison était petite.   *Our house was small.*
    Nous dormions quand le téléphone a sonné.   *We were sleeping when the
      telephone rang.*

# **Verbes** *Verbs*

## *The future*

The future expresses what will happen or what somebody will do.

It is formed by adding -**ai**, -**as**, -**a**, -**ons**, -**ez**, -**ont** to the infinitive. But -**re** verbs must drop the final **e** before adding the future ending, for example:

| donner | je donnerai | *I will give* |
| partir | elle partira | *she will leave* |
| écrire | vous écrirez | *you will write* |

The future can also be expressed by the following:
● the present tense: Qu'est-ce que tu fais demain?   *What are you doing tomorrow?*
● aller + infinitive: Je vais acheter une voiture.   *I am going to buy a car.*

## *Irregular verbs*

**Avoir** *to have*
Present: j'ai          nous avons
       tu as        vous avez
       il/elle/on a   ils/elles ont

Perfect:   j'ai eu
Imperfect:   j'avais
Future:   j'aurai

Expressions with **avoir**:

| J'ai vingt ans   *I am thirty* | J'ai du retard   *I am late* |
| J'ai chaud   *I am hot* | J'ai froid   *I am cold* |
| J'ai raison   *I am right* | J'ai tort   *I am wrong* |
| J'ai peur   *I am afraid* | J'ai le trac   *I am nervous* |
| J'ai mai à la tête   *I've got a headache* | |

**Être** *to be*
Present: je suis          nous sommes
       tu es          vous êtes
       il/elle/on est   ils/elles sont

Perfect:   j'ai été
Imperfect:   j'étais
Future:   je serai

# Verbes *Verbs*

**Aller** *to go*

| Present: | je vais | nous allons |
|---|---|---|
| | tu vas | vous allez |
| | il/elle/on va | ils/elles vont |

Perfect: je suis allé
Imperfect: j'allais
Future: j'irai

**Faire** *to do / make*

| Present: | je fais | nous faisons |
|---|---|---|
| | tu fais | vous faites |
| | il/elle/on fait | ils/elles font |

Perfect: j'ai fait
Imperfect: je faisais
Future: je ferai

(For more about irregular verbs see *Teach Yourself French Verbs*.)

## Reflexive verbs

These verbs have **me**, **te**, **se**, **nous** or **vous** between the subject pronoun and the verb, s'appeler *to be called* for example:

| je m'appelle | nous nous appelons |
|---|---|
| tu t'appelles | vous vous appelez |
| il/elle/on s'appelle | ils/elles s'appellent |

Common reflexive verbs: se réveiller *to wake up*; se lever *to get up*; se laver *to wash (oneself)*; s'habiller *to get dressed*; se promener *to go for a walk*; se souvenir de (quelque chose) *to remember (something)*; s'ennuyer *to be bored*; se passer *to happen*; se trouver *to be situated*.

Reflexive verbs form the perfect with **être**, for example elle s'est habillée *she got dressed*, nous nous sommes promenés *we went for a walk*.

## Question forms

Some questions are formed with question words (see page 23).
To form other questions you can:
- raise your intonation at the end of a statement: *Vous aimez la France?*
- put **est-ce que** before the statement: *Es-ce que vous aimez la France?*
- switch the position of the verb and the subject pronouns: *Aimez-vous la France?*

# Verbes *Verbs*

---

## *ENCORE!*

● *Activity: What did he do? What is he doing? What is he going to do?*

Yesterday                  Today                  Tomorrow

*And what did she do? What is she doing? What is she going to do?*

# 1 Les détails personnels *Personal matters*

## L'APPARENCE *APPEARANCE*

| | |
|---|---|
| Je suis ... | *I am ...* |
| Il / elle est ... | *He / she is ...* |
| grand(e) | *tall* |
| petit(e) | *short* |
| mince | *thin* |
| fort(e) } costaud } | *well-built* |
| gros(se) | *fat* |
| de taille moyenne | *medium height* |

| | |
|---|---|
| J'ai les cheveux ... | *I have ... hair* |
| foncés / clairs | *dark / fair* |
| acajou | *auburn* |
| roux / bruns / châtains | *red / brown / chestnut* |
| blonds | *blond* |
| gris / blancs | *grey / white* |
| longs / courts | *long / short* |
| raides / frisés | *straight / curly* |
| ondulés / clairsemés | *wavy / thinning* |
| et les yeux ... | *and ... eyes* |
| bleus | *blue* |
| bleu-gris | *blue-grey* |
| verts | *green* |
| bruns } marron } | *brown* |

| | |
|---|---|
| Je suis myope | *I am short-sighted* |
| astygmate | *long-sighted* |
| Je porte des lunettes | *I wear glasses* |
| des lentilles | *contact lenses* |
| Je suis beau / belle | *I am good-looking* |
| | *handsome* |

| | |
|---|---|
| la taille | *height* |
| Je mesure ... | *I am ... tall* |
| le poids | *weight* |
| Je pèse ... | *I weigh ...* |

# 1 **Les détails personnels** *Personal matters*

| | |
|---|---|
| J'ai la peau claire | *I am fair-skinned* |
| la peau mate | *dark-skinned* |
| un coup de soleil | *sunburned* |
| Je suis pâle | *I am pale* |
| Il / elle a ... | *He / she has ...* |
| une barbe | *a beard* |
| une moustache | *a moustache* |
| des tâches de rousseur (f. pl.) | *freckles* |
| des rides (f. pl.) | *wrinkles* |
| des fossettes (f. pl.) | *dimples* |
| une cicatrice | *a scar* |
| des boutons (m. pl.) | *spots* |
| de l'acné (f.) | *acne* |
| un grain de beauté | *a mole* |
| une tâche de naissance | *a birth mark* |
| un beau sourire | *a nice smile* |
| du ventre | *a beer belly* |
| un grand nez | *a big nose* |
| un petit nez rond | *a button nose* |
| un nez en trompette | *an upturned (retroussé) nose* |
| aquilin | *a roman nose* |
| cassé | *a broken nose* |
| épaté | *a boxer's nose* |
| des grandes / petites oreilles | *big / small ears* |
| des lèvres pulpeuses / minces | *thick / thin lips* |
| une grande / petite bouche | *a wide / narrow mouth* |
| un front haut | *a high forehead* |
| des sourcils en broussaille | *bushy eyebrows* |
| | |
| Il est chauve | *He has a bald head* |
| | |
| Il / elle est beau / belle | *He / she is pretty* |
| laid(e) | *ugly* |
| mignon(ne) | *cute* |
| charmant(e) | *sweet* |
| propre / sale | *clean / dirty* |
| négligé(e) / soigné(e) | *scruffy / well groomed* |
| beau / belle | *good-looking* |

| | |
|---|---|
| Elle est belle! | *Wow, she's a good looker!* |
| Il n'est pas mal (non plus). | *He's not bad (either)!* |

# 1 **Les détails personnels** *Personal matters*

---

## ENCORE!

- *Activity 1: Describe yourself.*

Je suis ＿＿＿＿＿＿

J'ai ＿＿＿＿＿＿

- *Activity 2: Fill in your details in French.*

### CURRICULUM VITAE

Nom (*Name*) ＿＿＿＿＿＿＿＿＿＿＿＿＿＿＿＿＿＿＿＿＿＿＿＿＿＿＿＿

Age (*Age*) ＿＿＿＿＿＿＿＿＿＿＿＿＿＿＿＿＿＿＿＿＿＿＿＿＿＿

Date de naissance (*Date of birth*) ＿＿＿＿＿＿＿＿＿＿＿＿＿＿＿

Lieu de naissance (*Place of birth*) ＿＿＿＿＿＿＿＿＿＿＿＿＿＿

Nationalité (*Nationality*) ＿＿＿＿＿＿＿＿＿＿＿＿＿＿＿＿＿＿

Formation (*Education / Training*) ＿＿＿＿＿＿＿＿＿＿＿＿＿＿

＿＿＿＿＿＿＿＿＿＿＿＿＿＿＿＿＿＿＿＿＿＿＿＿＿＿＿＿＿＿＿

Expérience professionnelle (*Work experience*) ＿＿＿＿＿＿＿＿＿

＿＿＿＿＿＿＿＿＿＿＿＿＿＿＿＿＿＿＿＿＿＿＿＿＿＿＿＿＿＿＿

Centres d'intérêt (*Interests*) ＿＿＿＿＿＿＿＿＿＿＿＿＿＿＿＿＿

# 1 Les détails personnels *Personal matters*

## LES SENTIMENTS
### *FEELINGS AND EMOTIONS*

| | |
|---|---|
| l'humeur (f.) | *mood* |
| l'émotion (f.) | *emotion* |
| le sentiment | *feeling* |

| | |
|---|---|
| dégouté(e) | *disgusted* |
| insatisfait(e) | *dissatisfied* |
| bouleversé(e) | *distressed* |
| exténué | *drained* |
| émotif (-ive) | *emotional* |
| enthousiaste | *enthusiastic* |

heureux    OK / pas mal    triste

| | |
|---|---|
| la peur | *fear* |
| l'anticipation (f.) | *anticipation* |
| la crainte | *dread* |
| la compassion | *compassion* |
| l'enthousiasme (m.) | *enthusiasm* |
| la sympathie | *sympathy* |
| le bonheur | *happiness* |
| l'optimisme (m.) | *optimism* |
| le pessimisme | *pessimism* |
| la tristesse | *sadness* |
| la dépression | *depression* |
| la gourmandise | *greed* |
| la satisfaction | *satisfaction* |
| l'insatisfaction (f.) | *dissatisfaction* |

| | |
|---|---|
| Je suis ... | *I feel ...* |
| effrayé(e) | *afraid* |
| en colère | *annoyed* |
| consterné(e) | *appalled* |
| appréhensif (-ive) | *apprehensive* |
| inquiet(-iète) | *concerned* |
| en forme | *cool!* |
| curieux (-ieuse) | *curious* |
| ravi(e) | *delighted* |
| déprimé(e) | *depressed* |

| | |
|---|---|
| envieux (-euse) | *envious* |
| crevé(e) | *exhausted* |
| en bonne condition physique | *fit* |
| amical(e) | *friendly* |
| super! | *great!* |
| heureux( -euse) | *happy* |
| plein(e) d'espoir | *hopeful* |
| malade | *ill* |
| de bonne humeur | *in a good mood* |
| relax | *laid back* |
| déçu(e) | *let down* |
| gai(e) | *lively* |
| chanceux (-euse) / malchanceux (-euse) | *lucky / unlucky* |
| rejeté(e) | *rejected* |
| décontracté(e) | *relaxed* |
| triste | *sad* |
| sexy | *sexy* |
| abattu(e) | *shattered* |
| surpris(e) | *suprised* |
| branché(e) | *switched on* |
| bavard(e) | *talkative* |
| en super / pleine forme | *terrific* |
| fatigué(e) | *tired* |

---

37

# 1 **Les détails personnels** *Personal matters*

| | | | | |
|---|---|---|---|---|
| dégoûté(e) | *turned off* | | en bonne | |
| malheureux | | | santé | *well* |
| (-euse) | *unhappy* | | dans le coup | *with it* |
| triste | *upset* | | soucieux (-euse) | *worried* |
| violent(e) | *violent* | | | |

| | |
|---|---|
| Ca va? | *How are you feeling?* |
| Je ne me sens pas bien | *I feel awful* |
| Je me sens mieux | *better* |
| plus mal | *worse* |
| Je suis de bonne / mauvaise humeur | *I am in a good / bad mood* |
| Il/elle sourit | *He / she is smiling* |
| pleure | *crying* |

# 1 Les détails personnels *Personal matters*

## LES TRAITS DE CARACTÈRE
### *CHARACTERISTICS*

Quel genre de personne es-tu?
(êtes-vous?)
*What sort of person are you?*

| Je suis ... | *I am ...* |
|---|---|
| dans la lune | *absent minded* |
| affectueux (-euse) | *affectionate* |
| ambitieux (-euse) | *ambitious* |
| coléreux (-euse) | *short-tempered* |
| arrogant(e) | *arrogant* |
| vantard(e) | *boastful* |
| ennuyeux (-euse) | *boring* |
| courageux (-euse) | *brave* |
| tyrannique | *bullying* |
| prudent(e) | *cautious* |
| charmant(e) | *charming* |
| de bonne humeur | *cheerful* |
| maladroit(e) | *clumsy* |
| vulgaire | *coarse* |
| compatissant(e) | *compassionate* |
| confiant(e) | *confident* |
| prévenant(e) | *considerate* |
| courageux (-euse) | *courageous* |
| cruel(le) | *cruel* |
| rusé(e) | *cunning* |
| curieux (-euse) | *curious, inquisitive* |
| envieux (-euse) | *envious* |
| indulgent(e) | *forgiving* |
| franc/franche | *frank* |
| sympathique | *friendly* |
| drôle | *funny* |
| généreux (-euse) | *generous* |
| doux/douce | *gentle* |
| courtois(e) | *gentlemanly* |
| gourmand(e) | *greedy* |
| heureux (-euse) | *happy* |
| travailleur (-euse) | *hard-working* |
| serviable | *helpful* |
| honnête | *honest* |
| plein(e) d'humour | *humorous* |
| impatient(e) | *impatient* |
| innocent(e) | *innocent* |
| insolent(e) | *insolent* |
| intelligent(e) | *intelligent* |
| irresponsable | *irresponsible* |
| jaloux (-ouse) | *jealous* |
| gentil(-le) | *kind* |
| distingué(e) | *ladylike* |
| paresseux (-euse) | *lazy* |
| espiègle | *mischievous* |
| radin(e) | *miserly* |
| pudique | *modest* |
| naïf / naïve | *naive* |
| méchant(e) | *nasty* |
| nerveux (-euse) | *nervous* |
| obstiné(e) | *obstinate* |
| ouvert(e) | *open* |
| autoritaire | *overbearing* |
| patient(e) | *patient* |
| agréable | *pleasant* |
| poli(e) | *polite* |
| fier / fière | *proud* |
| prudent(e) | *prudent* |
| tranquille | *quiet* |
| raisonnable | *reasonable* |
| raffiné(e) | *refined* |
| réservé(e) | *reserved* |

| | | | |
|---|---|---|---|
| respectueux | | plein(e) de | |
| (-euse) | *respectful* | tact | *tactful* |
| réticent(e) | *reticent* | timide | *timid* |
| abrupte | *rough* | tolérant(e) | *tolerant* |
| grossier | | digne de | |
| (-ière) | *rude* | confiance | *trustworthy* |
| secret (-ète) | *secretive* | vicieux (-euse) | *vicious* |
| sûr(e) de moi | *self-confident* | vindicatif | |
| égoïste | *selfish* | (-ive) | *vindictive* |
| sensible | *sensitive* | violent(e) | *violent* |
| sérieux (-euse) | *serious* | vulgaire | *vulgar* |
| perspicace | *shrewd* | bien élevé(e) { | *well-behaved* |
| sincère | *sincere* | | *well-educated* |
| méprisant(e) | *spiteful* | sage | *wise* |
| bizarre | *strange* | | |
| stupide | *stupid* | droitier (-ière) | *right-handed* |
| compatissant(e) | | gaucher (-ère) | *left-handed* |
| | *sympathetic* | | |

# 1 Les détails personnels *Personal matters*

## LES PRÉFÉRENCES
### *LIKES AND DISLIKES*

| | |
|---|---|
| J'aime | *I like* |
| Je n'aime pas | *I don't like* |
| J'aimerais | *I would like to* |
| Je préfère | *I prefer* |
| | |
| aimer | *to love* |

| | |
|---|---|
| admirer | *to admire* |
| adorer | *to adore* |
| être fan de ... | *to be a fan of ...* |
| aimer beaucoup | *to be fond of* |
| mépriser | *to despise* |
| haïr | *to hate* |
| détester | |
| avoir horreur de ... } | *to detest* |

---

## ENCORE!

● *Activity: What do they think?*

---

41

# 1 Les détails personnels *Personal matters*

## LA FAMILLE *FAMILY*

| | |
|---|---|
| l'arbre généalogique (m.) | |
| | *family tree* |
| la famille | *relations* |
| la famille proche | *close relations* |
| la famille éloignée | *distant relations* |
| les parents (m. pl.) | *parents / relations* |
| maternel(le) | *maternal* |
| paternel(le) | *paternal* |
| | |
| les arrière-grands-parents (m.pl.) | *great grandparents* |
| l'arrière-grand-mère | *great grandmother* |
| l'arrière-grand-père | *great grandfather* |
| | |
| les grands parents (m. pl.) | *grandparents* |
| la grand-mère | *grandmother* |
| la mamie | *grandma* |
| le grand-père | *grandfather* |
| le papie | *grandpa* |
| le petit-fils | *grandson* |
| la petite-fille | *granddaughter* |

| | |
|---|---|
| la mère | *mother* |
| la maman | *mum* |
| la belle-mère | *stepmother; mother-in-law* |
| le père | *father* |
| le papa | *dad* |
| le beau-père | *stepfather; father-in-law* |
| l'oncle (m.) | *uncle* |
| la tante | *aunt* |
| | |
| le fils | *son* |
| le gendre | *son-in-law* |
| la fille | *daughter* |
| la belle-fille | *daughter-in-law* |
| le frère | *brother* |
| le beau-frère | *brother-in-law* |
| la sœur | *sister* |
| la belle-sœur | *sister-in-law* |
| le demi-frère | *half-brother* |
| la demi-sœur | *half-sister* |
| le cousin | *cousin (male)* |
| la cousine | *cousin (female)* |
| | |
| l'adulte (m. f.) | *adult* |
| l'adolescent(e) | *adolescent* |
| l'enfant (m.f.) | *child* |
| le bébé | *baby* |

# 1 **Les détails personnels** *Personal matters*

| | | | |
|---|---|---|---|
| la marraine | *godmother* | jumelles | *identical twins* |
| le parrain | *godfather* | le couple marié | *married couple* |
| le filleul | *godson* | le fils unique | *only child (male)* |
| la filleule | *goddaughter* | la fille unique | *only child (female)* |
| | | adopté(e) | *adopted* |
| le frère aîné/ | *older / younger* | l'orphelin(e) | *orphan* |
| cadet | *brother* | | |
| la sœur aînée/ | *older / younger* | la photo | *photograph* |
| cadette | *sister* | l'album de | |
| le jumeau | *twin (male)* | photos (m.) | *photograph album* |
| la jumelle | *twin (female)* | Voilà une | |
| les vrais jumeaux/ | | photo de ... | *Here is a photo of* |

| | |
|---|---|
| J'aime ... | *I like ...* |
| Je n'aime pas ... | *I dislike ...* |
| Je m'entends bien/mal avec ... | *I get on well / badly with* |
| Je ne peux pas supporter ... | *I can't stand ...* |

## *ENCORE!*

● *Activity: Write in the names of the relations.*

# 1 **Les détails personnels** *Personal matters*

## LES ANIMAUX DOMESTIQUES
### *PETS*

| | |
|---|---|
| le chien | *dog* |
| le caniche | *poodle* |
| le berger allemand | *alsatian* |
| le labrador | *labrador* |
| le berger d'Écosse | *collie* |
| le chien d'aveugle | *guide dog* |
| le chien de garde | *guard dog* |

Attention! Chien méchant
*Beware of the dog*

| | |
|---|---|
| le chien de chasse | *hunting dog* |
| la niche | *dog kennel* |
| le panier | *dog basket* |
| la gamelle | *bowl* |
| le collier | *collar* |
| la laisse | *lead* |

Assis! Gentil!
*Sit! Good dog!*

| | |
|---|---|
| la nourriture | *food* |
| l'os (m.) | *bone* |
| la crotte de chien | *dog dirt* |
| le ramasse-crottes | *pooper scooper* |

Pelouse interdite aux chiens
*Dogs are not allowed to foul the grass*

| | |
|---|---|
| l'oiseau (m.) | *bird* |
| la perruche | *budgerigar* |
| le canari | *canary* |
| la cage | *cage* |
| les graines pour oiseaux (f. pl.) | *birdseed* |
| le chat | *cat* |
| la litière | *cat litter* |
| la porte pour chat | *cat flap* |
| le poisson rouge | *goldfish* |
| le poisson tropical | *tropical fish* |
| l'aquarium | *aquarium* |
| le bassin | *pond* |
| le cochon d'Inde | *guinea pig* |
| le hamster | *hamster* |
| la souris | *mouse* |
| le perroquet | *parrot* |
| le paon | *peacock* |
| le lapin | *rabbit* |
| nourrir<br>donner à manger à<br>donner à boire à | *to feed* |
| nettoyer | *to clean (out)* |
| emmener faire une promenade | *to take for a walk* |
| faire de l'exercice | *to exercise* |
| attraper | *to catch* |

## 2 La naissance, le mariage, la mort
### Birth, marriage and death

## Joyeux Anniversaire!
### Happy Birthday!

### LA NAISSANCE    BIRTH

| | |
|---|---|
| la naissance | birth |
| l'anniversaire (m.) | birthday |
| la date de naissance | date of birth |
| le bébé | baby |
| le garçon | boy |
| la fille | girl |
| la grossesse | pregnancy |
| le fœtus | foetus |
| l'utérus (m.) | womb |
| les contractions (f. pl.) | contractions |

| | |
|---|---|
| le travail | labour |
| la sage femme | midwife |
| le docteur | doctor |
| l'accouchement sans douleur (m.) | natural birth |
| la délivrance | delivery |
| les forceps (m. pl.) | forceps |
| la césarienne | caesarian |
| le baptême | christening, baptism |
| le nom | name |
| le parrain et la marraine | godparents |
| la marraine | godmother |
| le parrain | godfather |
| le cadeau | present / gift |

Felicitations! C'est un garçon!     *Congratulations! It's a boy!*
Felicitations! C'est une fille!     *Congratulations! It's a girl!*

## 2  La naissance, le mariage, la mort
### *Birth, marriage and death*

### LE BÉBÉ
### *BABY*

| | |
|---|---|
| les parents (m. pl.) | *parents* |
| la jeune fille au pair le jeune homme au pair | *au pair* |
| la nourrice | *childminder* |
| la gardienne la baby sitter | *baby sitter* |

| | |
|---|---|
| Je peux avoir ...? | *Can I have ...?* |
| J'ai besoin de ... | *I need ...* |
| Passe-moi ... | *Pass me ...* |
| le biberon | *baby's bottle* |
| la tétine | *teet* |
| le bain de bébé | *baby's bath* |
| la nourriture pour bébé | *baby food* |
| le trotte-bébé | *baby walker* |
| le bavoir | *bib* |
| le siège-auto | *car seat* |
| le linge | *cloth* |
| le berceau | *cot* |
| le drap pour le berceau | *cot sheet* |
| la couverture | *cot blanket* |
| la couette | *quilt* |
| la sucette | *dummy* |
| la chaise pour bébé | *high chair* |
| la berceuse | *lullaby* |
| le lait | *milk* |
| le mobile musical | *musical chimes* |
| la couche; le lange | *nappy* |
| la couche jetable | *disposable nappy* |
| l'épingle de sûreté (f.) | *nappy pin* |

| | |
|---|---|
| le pot | *potty* |
| le lait en poudre | *powdered milk* |
| le landeau | *pram* |
| la poussette | *push chair* |
| le hochet | *rattle* |
| la biscotte | *rusk* |
| la grenouillère | *sleeping suit* |
| la serviette | *towel* |
| les jouets (m. pl.) | *toys* |
| le maillot de corps | *vest* |
| les lingettes (f. pl.) | *wipes* |

| | |
|---|---|
| être né | *to be born* |
| Il/elle est né(e) | *He/she was born ...* |
| avoir un enfant | *to have a baby* |
| Elle a eu un bébé | *She has had a baby* |

| | |
|---|---|
| donner un bain | *to bath* |
| bouillir; stériliser | *to boil; sterilise* |
| donner le biberon | *to bottle feed* |
| allaiter | *to breast feed* |
| roter | *to burp* |
| changer la couche | *to change the nappy* |
| pleurer | *to cry* |
| nourrir | *to feed* |
| grandir | *to grow* |
| bercer | *to rock* |
| sourire | *to smile* |
| faire des dents | *to teethe* |
| (se) réveiller | *to wake up* |
| sevrer | *to wean* |
| essuyer | *to wipe* |
| s'endormir | *to get to sleep* |
| emmener le bébé faire une promenade | *to take the baby for a walk* |

# 2  La naissance, le mariage, la mort
*Birth, marriage and death*

---

| | |
|---|---|
| Il/elle pleure beaucoup | *He / she cries a lot* |
| ne dort pas | *doesn't sleep* |
| a mal au ... / à la | *has a sore ...* |

| | |
|---|---|
| J'ai besoin ... | *I need ...* |
| de crème pour fesses irritées | *cream for a sore bottom* |
| les coups de soleil | *for sunburn* |
| d'un médicament pour les maux d'estomac | *medicine for indigestion* |
| les dents qui percent | *teething* |
| une mauvaise toux | *a bad cough* |

| | |
|---|---|
| Qu'est-ce qu'il va mettre? | *What is he going to wear?* |
| À quelle heure mange-t-elle? | *When should she be fed?* |
| va-t-il dormir? | *he have a sleep?* |

---

## ENCORE!

● *Activity: Help the mother. What can't she find?*

---

47

# 2 La naissance, le mariage, la mort
## Birth, marriage and death

### GRANDIR
### GROWING UP

| | |
|---|---|
| le petit enfant | *infant* |
| le bambin | *toddler* |
| l'enfant *(m.f.)* | *child (m.f.)* |
| l'adolescent (e) | *adolescent (m.f.)* |
| la puberté | *puberty* |
| | |
| les jouets (m.pl.) | *toys* |

| | |
|---|---|
| la vidéo | *video* |
| la cassette | *cassette* |
| le tricycle | *tricycle* |
| la voiture à pédales | *toy car* |
| le vélo | *bicycle* |
| la poussette | *push chair* |
| s'asseoir | *to sit up* |
| marcher à quatre pattes | *to crawl* |

| | |
|---|---|
| Est-ce qu'il y a ...? | *Is there a ...?* |
| un jardin d'enfants | *children's playground* |
| une balançoire | *swing* |
| une cage à poule | *climbing frame* |
| un toboggan | *slide* |
| des manèges | *roundabouts* |
| | |
| C'est ...? | *Is it ...?* |
| sans danger | *safe* |
| dangereux | *dangerous* |
| adapté aux enfants de 3 ans | *suitable for 3-year-olds* |

| | |
|---|---|
| le coffre à jouets | *toy box* |
| les légos (m. pl.) | *building bricks* |
| le puzzle | *jigsaw* |
| les jeux d'éveil (m.pl.) | *early learning games* |
| les voitures en modèle réduit (f.pl.) | *model cars ...* |
| le livre d'histoires pour enfants (m. pl.) | *children's story book* |

| | |
|---|---|
| tomber | *to fall* |
| apprendre à marcher | *to learn to walk* |
| apprendre à parler | *to learn to talk* |
| jouer | *to play* |
| grandir | *to grow up* |

# 2 La naissance, le mariage, la mort
*Birth, marriage and death*

## AMOUR ET MARIAGE
### *LOVE AND MARRIAGE*

le petit ami — *boyfriend*
la petite amie — *girlfriend*
les fiançailles
(f. pl.) — *engagement*
le/la fiancé(e) — *fiancé(e)*
le partenaire — *partner*
le/la concubin(e) — *cohabitee*
la demande
en mariage — *proposal*
l'amant (m.) — *lover*
l'hétérosexuel
(-elle) — *heterosexual*
l'homosexuel
(-elle) — *homosexual*
la lesbienne — *lesbian*

s'aimer — *to love each other*
tomber
amoureux — *to fall in love*
se fiancer — *to get engaged*
sortir ensemble — *to go out together*
coucher
ensemble — *to sleep together*
avoir des rapports
sexuels — *to have sex*

la demoiselle
d'honneur — *maid of honour*
la lune de miel — *honeymoon*
la mairie — *registry office*
l'alliance (f.) — *wedding ring*
le mari — *husband*
la femme — *wife*
l'invitation (f.) — *invitation*
le mariage — *wedding*
le jour du
mariage — *wedding day*

les jeunes
mariés (m. pl.) *newly weds*
les noces
d'argent/d'or *silver / gold*
(f. pl.) *wedding*

### Le mariage *Marriage*

Félicitations pour le mariage!
*Congratulations on your wedding day!*

le certificat — *certificate*
la cérémonie — *ceremony*
le mariage
religieux — *church wedding*
le mariage civil — *civil marriage*
la mariée — *bride*
le marié — *groom*
le témoin — *best man*

la situation
familiale — *marital status*
Je suis ... — *I am ...*
célibataire — *single*
marié(e) — *married*
divorcé(e) — *divorced*
séparé(e) — *separated*
vieux garçon — *batchelor*
vieille fille — *spinster*
Je vis avec — *I'm living with*
quelqu'un — *a partner*

# 2 La naissance, le mariage, la mort
## Birth, marriage and death

| | | | |
|---|---|---|---|
| le nom de jeune fille | maiden name | le divorce | divorce |
| le nom | surname; married name | se marier | to get married |
| | | se séparer | to get separated |
| la séparation | separation | divorcer | to divorce |

## LA MORT  *DEATH*

| | |
|---|---|
| Mon mari est mort | My husband has died |
| Ma femme est morte | My wife has died |
| Mon ami(e) est mort(e) | My friend has died |
| Je suis veuve | I am a widow |
| veuf | widower |
| en deuil | bereaved; in mourning |

| | | | |
|---|---|---|---|
| les funérailles (f. pl.) | funeral | le convoi funèbre | mourners |
| l'enterrement (m.) | burial | être en deuil | to be in mourning |
| le cimetière | cemetery | le testament | will |
| le cercueil | coffin | l'héritier | heir |
| la crémation | cremation | l'héritière | heiress |
| la tombe | grave | hériter | to inherit |

| | |
|---|---|
| mourir | to die |
| avoir une attaque | to have a stroke |
| faire une crise cardiaque | to have a heart attack |
| avoir le cancer | to have cancer |
| être tué(e) dans un accident | to be killed in an accident |
| se suicider | to commit suicide |
| se tuer | to kill one self |
| être empoisonné(e) | to be poisoned |
| enterrer | to bury |
| porter le deuil | to mourn |
| présenter ses condoléances | to convey one's condolences |

# 2 La naissance, le mariage, la mort
## *Birth, marriage and death*

**M. Joseph LUBRANO
di SCAMPAMORTE**
chevalier
de la Légion d'honneur,

survenu dans sa 97ᵉ année,
le 15 mai 1996.

La cérémonie religieuse
aura lieu le samedi 18 mai,
à 10 heures, en l'abbaye de
Saint-Victor, à Marseille.

On nous prie de faire part
du décès, dans sa 98ᵉ année,
de

**Mme veuve
Jean WAMPFLER**
née Henriette Boutin.

Les obsèques
ont eu lieu dans l'intimité
le 10 mai 1996.

| | |
|---|---|
| Toutes mes condoléances | *I would like to convey my condolences* |
| Je suis désolé(e) d'apprendre la triste nouvelle | *I am very sorry to learn of your sad loss* |

# 3 Les vêtements et la mode *Clothes and fashion*

## LA MODE *FASHION*

| | | | |
|---|---|---|---|
| la présentation | | le commentateur | *commentator* |
| de mode | *fashion show* | le photographe | *photographer* |
| de collection | | le journaliste | |
| le défilé de mode | *cat walk* | de mode | *fashion journalist* |
| le mannequin | *model* | Ramon porte... | *Ramon is wearing ...* |
| le grand | | Sylvie porte... | *Sylvie is wearing ...* |
| couturier | *designer* | le client/la cliente | *client* |

Ramon porte un pantalon bleu,
une chemise à carreaux rouges et
blancs et un pullover bleu-foncé,
des chaussettes jaunes et des
baskets blanches.

Sylvie porte un chemisier blanc,
une jupe noire avec une écharpe
rouge, des boucles d'oreilles en or,
des collants blancs et des chaussures
rouges à hauts talons.

# 3 Les vêtements et la mode *Clothes and fashion*

## LES VÊTEMENTS
### *CLOTHES*

### Les vêtements de tous les jours *Everyday wear*

| | |
|---|---|
| porter | *to wear* |
| mettre | *to put on* |
| enlever | *to take off* |
| s'habiller | *to get dressed* |
| se changer | *to change* |
| se déshabiller | *to get undressed* |
| essayer | *to try on* |

| | |
|---|---|
| le tablier | *apron* |
| la ceinture | *belt* |
| le chemisier | *blouse* |
| les bretelles (f.pl.) | *braces* |
| le gilet | *cardigan* |
| le foulard | *cravat; headscarf* |
| le smoking | *dinner jacket* |
| la robe de chambre | *dressing gown* |
| la robe du soir | *evening dress* |
| le jean | *jeans* |
| le pull(-over) | *jumper* |
| le caleçon | *leggings* |
| le polo | *polo shirt* |
| le pull à col roulé | *roll neck sweater* |
| la chemise | *shirt* |
| le short | *shorts* |
| la jupe | *skirt* |
| les chaussettes (f.pl.) | *socks* |
| les bas (m.pl.) | *stockings* |
| le costume | *man's suit* |
| le tailleur | *woman's suit* |
| le sweat-(shirt) | *sweatshirt* |
| le tee-shirt | *t-shirt* |

| | |
|---|---|
| la cravate | *tie* |
| le/les collant(s) | *tights* |
| le pantalon | *trousers* |
| le gilet | *waistcoat* |
| l'uniforme (m.) | *uniform* |

### Les sous-vêtements *Underwear*

| | |
|---|---|
| le body | *body* |
| le soutien-gorge | *bra* |
| le slip | *briefs* |
| la culotte | *knickers* |
| le jupon | *petticoat, underskirt* |
| la combinaison | *slip* |
| le collant | *tights* |
| le caleçon | *underpants* |
| le maillot de corps | *vest* |
| le porte-jarretelles | *suspender belt* |
| la gaine | *girdle* |

### Les vêtements de dessus *Outerwear*

| | |
|---|---|
| l'anorak (m.) | *anorak* |
| la casquette (de baseball) | *(baseball) cap* |
| le manteau | *coat* |
| les gants (m.pl.) | *gloves* |
| le chapeau | *hat* |
| le foulard | *headscarf* |
| la capuche | *hood* |
| la veste | *jacket* |
| l'imperméable (m.) | *raincoat* |
| l'écharpe (f.) | *scarf* |
| le parapluie | *umbrella* |
| le bonnet | *woolly hat* |

# 3  Les vêtements et la mode *Clothes and fashion*

## Les vêtements de sport
### *Sportswear*

| | |
|---|---|
| le cycliste | *cycling shorts* |
| le collant | *leotard* |
| le short | *shorts* |
| le survêtement | } *tracksuit* |
| le jogging | |
| le bikini | *bikini* |

## LES CHAUSSURES
### *FOOTWEAR*

| | |
|---|---|
| les bottes (f.pl.) | *boots* |
| les palmes (f.pl.) | *flippers* |
| les chaussures de foot (f.pl.) | *football boots* |
| les chaussures à hauts talons (f.pl.) | *high-heeled shoes* |
| les chaussures à lacets (f.pl.) | *lace-ups* |
| les bottes en caoutchouc | *rubber boots* |

| | |
|---|---|
| le maillot (de bain) | *swimming costume / trunks* |
| le maillot une pièce | *swimsuit* |
| le slip de bain | *trunks* |
| le bonnet de bain | *swim hat* |
| la combinaison de plongée | *wet suit* |
| les sandales (f.pl.) | *sandals* |
| les chaussures (f.pl.) | *shoes* |
| les chaussures de ski (f.pl.) | *ski boots* |
| les pantoufles (f.pl.) | *slippers* |
| les chaussettes (f.pl.) | *socks* |
| les baskets (f.pl.) | *trainers* |
| la paire de... | *pair of...* |

---

## *ENCORE!*

● *Activity: What are they wearing?*

(a) Il pleut!　　　　　　　　(b) Il fait chaud!

# 3 Les vêtements et la mode *Clothes and fashion*

## LES PARTIES DU VÊTEMENT
### *PARTS OF THE GARMENT*

| | |
|---|---|
| la boutonnière | *buttonhole* |
| le corsage | *bodice* |
| le col | *collar* |
| les poignets (m.pl.) | *cuffs* |
| la pince | *dart* |
| l'ourlet (m.) | *hem* |
| le revers | *lapel; turn-up* |
| le plis | *pleat* |
| la couture | *seam* |
| la manche | *sleeve* |

## Les tissus *Materials*

| | |
|---|---|
| le coton | *cotton* |
| le denim | *denim* |
| la feutrine | *felt* |
| le jersey | *jersey* |
| la dentelle | *lace* |
| le lin | *linen* |
| le nylon | *nylon* |
| le polyester | *polyester* |
| le ruban | *ribbon* |
| le satin | *satin* |
| la soie | *silk* |
| le daim | *suede* |
| le tweed | *tweed* |
| le velours | *velvet* |
| la laine | *wool* |
| | |
| la fourrure | *fur* |
| le cuir | *leather* |
| le plastique | *plastic* |
| le caoutchouc | *rubber* |

## Les notions de couture
### *Sewing*

Un point à temps en vaut cent.
*A stitch in time saves nine.*

| | |
|---|---|
| le bouton | *button* |
| le col | *collar* |
| le poignet | *cuff* |
| l'attache (f.) | *fastener* |
| l'ourlet (m.) | *hem* |
| le revers | *lapel* |
| l'aiguille (f.) | *needle* |
| l'épingle (f.) | *pin* |
| la poche | *pocket* |
| l'épingle de sûreté (f.) | *safety pin* |
| les ciseaux (m.pl.) | *scissors* |
| la machine à coudre | *sewing machine* |
| la manche | *sleeve* |
| le fil | *thread* |
| la fermeture éclair | *zip* |
| le patron | *pattern* |

## Les styles *Styles*

| | |
|---|---|
| large | *baggy* |
| sport | *casual* |
| à carreaux | *checked* |
| classique | *classical* |
| froissé(e) | *crumpled* |
| à la mode | *fashionable* |
| à fleurs | *floral* |
| habillé(e) | *formal* |
| mal assorti(e) | *ill-matching* |
| long(ue) | *long* |
| prêt-à-porter | *off-the-peg* |
| à motifs | *patterned* |
| uni(e) | *plain* |

# 3 Les vêtements et la mode *Clothes and fashion*

| | | | |
|---|---|---|---|
| plissé(e) | *pleated* | écossais(e) | *tartan* |
| imprimé(e) | *printed* | étroit(e) | *tight* |
| court(e) | *short* | serré(e) | |
| élégant(e) | *smart* | faire des | |
| à pois | *spotted* | modifications | *to alter* |
| à rayures | *striped* | changer | *to change* |

**L'ENTRETIEN DES
VÊTEMENTS**
*CLOTHING CARE*

| | | | |
|---|---|---|---|
| | | nettoyer à sec | *to dry clean* |
| | | suspendre | *to hang up (a suit)* |
| le ceintre | *coat hanger* | repasser | *to iron* |
| la patère | *coat hook* | rallonger | *to lengthen* |
| le ceintre pince | *skirt hanger* | faire | *to make* |
| le fer à repasser | *iron* | réparer | *to mend* |
| le fer à vapeur | *steam iron* | repasser | *to press* |
| la presse | *trouser press* | coudre | *to sew* |
| | | raccourcir | *to shorten* |
| nettoyer | *to clean* | tacher | *to stain* |
| | | déchirer | *to tear* |
| | | attacher | *to tie* |

## ENCORE!

● *Activity: What are they packing?*

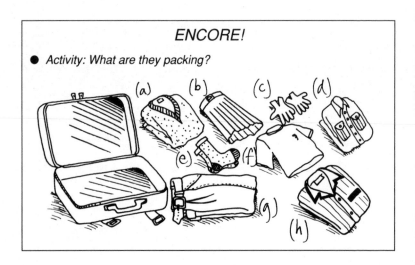

# 3 Les vêtements et la mode *Clothes and fashion*

| | | |
|---|---|---|
| Lavage ou nettoyage à sec? | | *Wash or dry clean?* |
| Instructions de lavage | | *Washing symbols* |
| Nettoyage à sec | (P) | *Dry clean only* |
| Lavage à main | | *Handwash only* |
| Laver séparément | | *Wash separately* |
| Lavage à l'eau tiède | | *Use tepid water* |
| Ne pas mettre dans un séchoir électrique | | *Do not tumble dry* |
| Javel interdite | | *Do not use bleach* |
| Ne pas repasser | | *Do not iron* |
| Fer tiède | | *Use only cool iron* |
| Ne pas amidonner | | *Do not use starch* |
| Séchage à plat | | *Dry flat* |
| Cet article déteint au lavage | | *This product will lose colour when washed* |
| Ne pas laisser tremper | | *Do not soak* |
| Ne pas utiliser de détergents | | *Do not use detergent* |
| Essuyer avec un linge humide | | *Wipe with a damp cloth* |

# 3 Les vêtements et la mode *Clothes and fashion*

## LES ACCESSOIRES
### *ACCESSORIES*

| | |
|---|---|
| le sac à main | *handbag* |
| le sac à bandoulière | *shoulder bag* |
| le porte-monnaie | *purse* |
| le parapluie | *umbrella* |
| la ceinture | *belt* |
| les gants (m.pl.) | *gloves* |
| l'écharpe (f.) | *scarf* |
| le châle | *shawl* |
| la montre | *watch* |

## Les bijoux *Jewellery*

| | |
|---|---|
| le bracelet | *bracelet* |
| la broche | *brooch* |
| la chaîne | *chain* |
| les bijoux fantaisie (m.pl.) | *costume jewellery* |
| la croix | *cross* |
| les boutons de manchettes (m.pl.) | *cuff links* |
| les boucles d'oreilles (f.pl.) | *earrings* |
| se faire percer les oreilles | *to have one's ears pierced* |
| le collier | *necklace* |
| l'anneau pour le nez (m.) | *nose ring* |
| le pendentif | *pendant* |

| | |
|---|---|
| la bague | *ring* |
| l'alliance (f.) | *wedding ring* |
| la bague de fiançailles | *engagement ring* |
| la chevalière | *signet ring* |
| le tatouage | *tattoo* |
| la tiare | *tiara* |
| l'épingle à cravate (f.) | *tie pin* |
| la montre | *watch* |

## Les pierres précieuses ou semi-précieuses
### *Precious and semi-precious stones*

Les diamants sont éternels!
*Diamonds are forever!*

| | |
|---|---|
| l'améthyste (f.) | *amethyst* |
| le bronze | *bronze* |
| le cuivre | *copper* |
| le corail | *coral* |
| le cristal | *crystal* |
| le diamant | *diamond* |
| l'émeraude (f.) | *emerald* |
| l'émail (m.) | *enamel* |
| l'or (m.) | *gold* |
| l'opale (f.) | *opal* |
| la perle | *pearl* |
| le rubis | *ruby* |
| le saphir | *sapphire* |
| l'argent (m.) | *silver* |
| le bois | *wood* |

# 3 Les vêtements et la mode *Clothes and fashion*

## Le parfum  *Perfume*

| | |
|---|---|
| la lavande | *lavender* |
| fleuri | *flowery* |
| l'eau de toilette (f.) | *toilet water* |

| | |
|---|---|
| le parfum | *scent, perfume* |
| l'atomiseur (m.) | *spray* |

## ENCORE!

● *Activity  What are they going to buy?*

# 4 Manger et boire  *Food and drink*

À table
*Come and eat!*

## Mettre la table
### *Laying the table*

| | |
|---|---|
| le couteau | *knife* |
| la fourchette | *fork* |
| la cuillère | *spoon* |
| la grande cuillère | *serving spoon* |
| le set de table | *place mat* |
| les condiments (m.pl.) | *condiments* |
| le sel | *salt* |
| le poivre | *pepper* |
| l'huile (f.) | *salad oil* |
| le vinaigre | *vinegar* |
| la sauce tomate | *tomato sauce* |
| la sauce de soja | *soya sauce* |
| l'assiette (f.) | *plate* |
| la tasse | *cup* |
| la soucoupe | *saucer* |
| le plat | *dish* |
| la théière | *teapot* |
| la carafe; le pichet | *jug* |
| le verre | *glass* |
| le bol | *bowl* |
| la cafetière | *coffee pot* |
| la bouteille | *bottle* |

## Les repas  *Meals*

| | |
|---|---|
| le petit déjeuner | *breakfast* |
| le déjeuner | *lunch* |
| le dîner | *dinner* |
| le goûter | *tea* |
| le souper | *supper* |
| le casse-croûte | *snack* |

## LA NOURRITURE
### *FOOD*

## Le petit déjeuner  *Breakfast*

| | |
|---|---|
| les céréales (f.pl.) | *cereal* |
| le pamplemousse | *grapefruit* |
| la salade de fruits | *fruit salad* |
| le jus d'orange | *orange juice* |
| une tranche de pain | *a slice of bread* |
| la confiture | *jam* |
| la crêpe | *pancake* |
| le sirop d'érable | *maple syrup* |
| le pain grillé | *toast* |
| la margarine | *margarine* |
| le beurre | *butter* |
| la marmelade | *marmalade* |
| le muesli | *müesli* |
| le miel | *honey* |
| le fromage | *cheese* |
| le jambon | *ham* |
| la crème | *cream* |

# 4 Manger et boire *Food and drink*

## La viande *Meat*

| | |
|---|---|
| le bœuf | *beef* |
| le veau | *veal* |
| le porc | *pork* |
| le mouton | *mutton* |
| l'agneau (m.) | *lamb* |
| la volaille | *poultry* |
| la dinde | *turkey* |
| le canard | *duck* |
| l'oie (f.) | *goose* |
| le faisan | *pheasant* |
| la bécasse | *snipe, woodcock* |
| la caille | *quail* |
| le venaison | *venison* |
| le lapin | *rabbit* |
| le lièvre | *hare* |

| | |
|---|---|
| la viande hachée | *minced meat* |
| un steak haché | *minced steak (usually reformed for burgers, etc.)* |
| la saucisse | *sausage* |
| le steak | *steak* |
| la côte (de porc, d'agneau) | *chop (pork, lamb)* |
| les escargots (m.pl.) | *snails* |

## Le poisson *Fish*

| | |
|---|---|
| le poisson fumé | *smoked fish* |
| le poisson d'eau douce | *freshwater fish* |
| la truite | *trout* |
| la perche | *perch* |
| le saumon | *salmon* |
| le gardon | *roach* |

| | |
|---|---|
| le poisson d'eau de mer | *sea fish* |
| la morue | *cod* |

| | |
|---|---|
| le maquereau | *mackerel* |
| le hareng | *herring* |
| le thon | *tuna* |
| le poulpe | *octopus* |
| le requin | *shark* |
| l'encornet (m.) la seiche | *squid* |
| le merlan | *whiting* |

| | |
|---|---|
| les crustacés (m.pl.) | *shellfish* |
| le crabe | *crab* |
| le homard | *lobster* |
| la crevette | *shrimp* |
| la crevette rose | *prawn* |
| la langoustine | *langoustine* |
| les moules (f.pl.) | *mussels* |
| les coques (f.pl.) | *cockles* |
| les coquilles Saint-Jacques (f.pl.) | *scallops* |

## Le pain *Bread*

| | |
|---|---|
| les pains briochés / les petits pains (m.pl.) | *bread buns / rolls* |
| les croissants (m.pl.) | *croissants* |
| le pain | *white bread* |
| le pain au son | *brown bread* |
| le pain complet | *wholemeal bread* |
| le pain de seigle | *rye bread* |
| les biscuits à fromage (m.pl.) | *crackers* |

## Les fruits et légumes *Fruit and vegetables*

| | |
|---|---|
| la pomme | *apple* |
| l'abricot (m.) | *apricot* |

# 4 Manger et boire  *Food and drink*

| | |
|---|---|
| la banane | *banana* |
| la mûre | *blackberry* |
| la cerise | *cherry* |
| la canneberge | *cranberry* |
| la groseille | *redcurrant* |
| la groseille à maquereau | *gooseberry* |
| le pamplemousse | *grapefruit* |
| le kiwi | *kiwi* |
| le citron | *lemon* |
| le citron vert | *lime* |
| la mangue | *mango* |
| le melon | *melon* |
| l'orange (f.) | *orange* |
| la pêche | *peach* |
| la poire | *pear* |
| la framboise | *raspberry* |
| la fraise | *strawberry* |
| la prune | *plum* |
| le cassis | *blackcurrant* |
| | |
| la pomme de terre | *potato* |
| l'oignon (m.) | *onion* |
| les échalottes (f.pl.) | *shallots* |
| l'ail (m.) | *garlic* |
| le poireau | *leek* |
| les petits pois (m.pl.) | *peas* |
| le haricot | *bean* |
| le haricot rouge | *kidney bean* |
| la fève | *broad bean* |
| les haricots verts | *green beans, French beans* |
| le chou | *cabbage* |

| | |
|---|---|
| le chou rouge | *red cabbage* |
| le chou-fleur | *cauliflower* |
| les choux de Bruxelles (m.pl.) | *Brussels sprouts* |
| la carotte | *carrot* |
| le brocoli | *broccoli* |
| la courgette | *courgette* |
| le panais | *parsnip* |
| le navet | *turnip* |
| le cresson | *watercress* |
| le poivron | *pepper* |
| les fines herbes (f.pl.) | *herbs* |
| la ciboulette | *chives* |
| le persil | *parsley* |
| le fenouil | *fennel* |
| le romarin | *rosemary* |
| le basilic | *basil* |
| les herbes de Provence (f.pl.) | *herbs of Provence* |
| le thym | *thyme* |
| | |
| grillé | *grilled* |
| cru | *raw* |
| cuit | *cooked* |
| | |
| les pommes de terre (f.pl.) | *potatoes* |
| cuites au four | *baked* |
| rôties | *roast* |
| à la crème | *creamed* |
| en purée | *mashed* |
| à l'eau | *boiled* |
| les frites (f.pl.) | *chips* |

# 4 Manger et boire  *Food and drink*

## LES BOISSONS
### *DRINKS*

### Les boissons chaudes
*Hot drinks*

| | |
|---|---|
| une tasse de ... | *a cup of ...* |
| avec du lait | *with milk* |
| du citron | *lemon* |
| de la crème | *cream* |
| le sucre | *sugar* |
| des sucrettes (f.) ⎫ | *artificial* |
| un édulcorant ⎭ | *sweetener(s)* |
| la soucoupe | *saucer* |
| la petite cuillère | *teaspoon* |
| le thé | *tea* |
| la tisane | *fruit tea / tisane* |
| l'églantine (f.) | *rosehip* |
| la verveine | *verbena* |
| la camomille | *chamomile* |
| le sachet de thé | *tea-bag* |
| le café | *coffee* |
| le nescafé | *instant coffee* |
| le café crème | *milky coffee* |
| un déca | *decaffeinated coffee* |
| un cappuccino | *cappuccino* |
| un expresso | *espresso* |
| un chocolat chaud | *hot chocolate* |
| un café crème | *a milky coffee* |

### Les boissons fraîches
*Cold drinks*

| | |
|---|---|
| les boissons gazeuses (f.pl.) | *minerals* |
| un verre | *a glass* |
| deux verres de bière | *two glasses of beer* |
| une boîte/une cannette | *a can* |

| | |
|---|---|
| une bouteille/ une demie-bouteille | *a bottle / half bottle* |
| une brique | *a carton* |
| de l'eau | *water* |
| de l'eau/ minérale | *mineral water* |
| pétillante ⎫ gazeuse ⎭ | *sparkling* |
| plate | *still* |
| la limonade | *lemonade* |
| l'orangeade (f.) | *orangeade* |
| le coca | *Coca-Cola* |
| le jus de fruits | *fruit juice* |
| de pomme | *apple* |
| de pamplemousse | *grapefruit* |
| d'orange | *orange* |
| de cassis | *blackcurrant* |
| d'abricot | *apricot* |
| d'ananas | *pineapple* |

### Les alcools  *Alcoholic drinks*

| | |
|---|---|
| la bière | *beer* |
| la bière blonde | *lager (light)* |
| la bière brune | *stout (dark)* |
| un demi | *a glass of beer (roughly half a pint)* |
| une pression | *draught beer* |
| le vin | *wine* |
| rouge | *red* |
| blanc | *white* |
| rosé | *rosé* |
| le champagne | *champagne* |
| le vin de table | *house wine / table wine* |
| le cognac | *brandy* |
| le whisky | *whisky* |
| le rhum | *rum* |
| la vodka | *vodka* |
| le gin | *gin* |

# 4 **Manger et boire** *Food and drink*

| | | |
|---|---|---|
| boire | *to drink* | À votre santé! |
| siroter/boire | | *Cheers! Good health!* |
| une gorgée | *to sip* | |

## ENCORE!

● *Activity: What would you say to order these drinks?*

Je voudrais …

# 4 Manger et boire  *Food and drink*

## DANS LA CUISINE
### *IN THE KITCHEN*

| | |
|---|---|
| le chef | *chef* |
| le cuisinier | *cook* |
| le plongeur | *washer-upper* |

## Les ingrédients  *Ingredients*

| | |
|---|---|
| la farine | *flour* |
| la farine pour gâteaux | *self-raising flour* |
| la farine de blé | *plain flour* |
| la maïzena/ la farine de maïs | *cornflour* |
| la fécule de pomme de terre | *potato flour* |
| les levures (f.pl.) | *baking powder* |
| la levure de boulanger | *yeast* |
| la levure chimique | *bicarbonate of soda* |
| le sucre | *sugar* |
| le sucre glace | *icing sugar* |
| le sucre brun | *brown sugar* |
| les matières grasses (f.pl.) | *fats* |
| la margarine | *margarine* |
| l'huile (f.) | *oil* |
| l'huile d'olive | *olive oil* |
| l'huile de tournesol | *sunflower oil* |
| l'huile d'arachide | *groundnut / peanut oil* |
| les produits laitiers | *dairy products* |
| le fromage | *cheese* |
| le beurre | *butter* |
| la crème | *cream* |
| le lait | *milk* |
| la crème fraîche | *sour cream* |

| | |
|---|---|
| le yaourt | *yoghurt* |
| le fromage frais/blanc | *'fromage frais'* |
| demi-écrémé | *half fat* |
| entier | *full fat* |
| le fromage fondu | *processed cheese* |
| l'œuf | *egg* |
| le jaune d'œuf | *yolk* |
| le blanc | *white* |
| les fruits secs (m.pl.) | *dried fruit* |
| les raisins secs (m.pl.) | *raisins* |
| les raisins de Corinthe | *sultanas* |
| la figue | *fig* |
| la datte | *date* |
| les cerises confites (f.pl.) | *glacé cherries* |
| les noix (f.) | *nuts* |
| l'amande (f.) | *almond* |
| la noisette | *hazel nut* |
| la noix de cajou | *cashew nut* |
| des noisettes en poudre | *ground hazelnuts* |
| la noix | *walnut* |
| la noix de coco | *coconut* |
| la cacahuète | *peanut* |
| la pistache | *pistachio* |
| les amandes effilées | *flaked almonds* |

## Les ustensiles de cuisine
### *Cooking utensils*

| | |
|---|---|
| la plaque de four | *baking tray* |
| la planche à découper | *chopping board* |
| la planche à pain | *bread board* |
| l'ouvre-bouteille (m.) | *bottle opener* |

# 4 Manger et boire  *Food and drink*

| | |
|---|---|
| le saladier | *bowl* |
| le moule à gâteaux | *cake tin* |
| le couteau et la fourchette à découper la viande | *carving knife and fork* |
| la passoire | *colander* |
| le tire-bouchon | *corkscrew* |
| la roulette à découper; un emporte-pièce | *}biscuit / pastry cutter* |
| la poêle à frire | *frying pan* |
| le couteau de cuisine | *kitchen knife* |
| les gants (m.pl.) pour le four isolants | *}oven gloves* |
| le plat à rôtir | *roasting tin* |
| le rouleau à pâtisserie | *rolling pin* |
| la casserole | *saucepan* |
| les ciseaux (m.pl.) | *scissors* |
| l'aiguisoir (m.) | *sharpener* |
| le tamis | *sieve* |
| l'ouvre-boîte (m.) | *tin opener* |
| les balances ménagères (f.pl.) | *weighing scales* |
| le fouet | *whisk* |

| | |
|---|---|
| le batteur | *electric whisk* |
| la cuillère en bois | *wooden spoon* |
| la cafetière | *coffee machine* |
| le grill | *grill* |
| la plaque électrique/ le brûleur | *hob (electric / gas)* |
| le mixeur | *mixer* |
| le robot | *food processor* |
| le thermostat | *thermostat* |
| le sablier/le compte-minutes | *egg-timer* |
| le grille-pain | *toaster* |
| le micro-ondes | *microwave* |

| | |
|---|---|
| cuire au four | *to bake* |
| arroser | *to baste* |
| battre | *to beat* |
| (faire) bouillir | *to boil* |
| (faire) fondre | *to melt* |
| braiser | *to braise* |
| cuire | *to cook* |
| frire | *to fry* |
| griller | *to grill* |
| mélanger | *to mix* |
| rôtir | *to roast* |
| cuire à la vapeur | *to steam* |
| laisser mijoter | *to stew* |
| cuire à feux doux | *to simmer* |
| remuer | *to stir* |
| égoutter | *to strain* |

| | |
|---|---|
| Bon appétit! | *Enjoy your meal!* |
| À toi aussi! À vous aussi! | *And you too!* |
| J'aime ... | *I like...* |
| Je n'aime pas ... | *I don't like ...* |
| J'ai assez mangé. | *I'm full.* |
| C'est bon! | *It's good!* |
| trop chaud | *too hot* |
| trop sucré | *too sweet* |
| trop amer | *too sour* |
| trop | *too much* |
| trop froid | *too cold* |

## 4 Manger et boire  *Food and drink*

### MANGER EN VILLE
#### *EATING OUT*

| | |
|---|---|
| le fast food/ la cuisine rapide | *fast food* |
| le snack-bar | *snack bar* |
| le café | *café* |
| le bar | *bar* |
| le restaurant | *restaurant* |
| la pizzéria | *pizzeria* |
| la crêperie | *creperie* |
| la saladerie | *salad bar* |
| le self | *self service restaurant* |
| la cantine | *canteen* |
| la cafétéria | *cafeteria* |
| la brasserie | *cafe in which light meals or snacks are served* |
| le pub anglais | *pub* |

### Au restaurant
#### *At the restaurant*

| | |
|---|---|
| la table | *table* |
| le cendrier | *ashtray* |
| le cure-dent | *toothpick* |
| la chaise | *chair* |
| une place libre | *a free (vacant) place* |
| le couvert | *a place setting* |
| les condiments (m.pl.) | *condiments* |
| l'huile (f.) | *oil* |
| le vinaigre | *vinegar* |
| les cornichons (m.pl.) | *gherkins* |
| les olives (f.pl.) | *olives* |
| le menu (à 110FF) | *a 'set' meal (at 110FF)* |

| | |
|---|---|
| la sauce | *sauce* |
| la moutarde | *mustard* |
| les couverts (m.pl.) | *cutlery* |
| une carafe d'eau | *a jug of water* |
| la serviette | *napkin* |
| le rince-doigts | *finger bowl* |
| le serveur | *waiter* |
| la serveuse | *waitress* |
| le sommelier | *wine waiter* |
| le couvert | *cover charge* |
| la T.V.A. | *VAT* |
| Toutes Taxes Comprises (T.T.C) | *all charges included; all-inclusive* |
| le service | *service charge* |
| le pourboire | *tip* |
| l'addition (f.) | *bill* |
| le reçu | *receipt* |
| la monnaie | *change* |
| le plat du jour | *meal of the day, dish* |
| la carte | *menu* |
| le hors d'œuvre/ l'entrée (f.) | *starter / first course* |
| le plat de poisson | *fish course* |
| le plat de résistance | *main course* |
| le dessert | *dessert* |
| la salade | *salad* |
| le fromage | *cheese* |
| les fruits (m.pl.) | *fruit* |
| les pâtisseries (f.pl.) | *tarts / cakes* |
| les glaces (f.pl.) | *ice creams* |

# 5  La maison et le jardin *Home and garden*

## LE LOGEMENT  *ACCOMMODATION*

| | | | |
|---|---|---|---|
| la maison | *house* | un endroit | *quiet /* |
| individuelle | *detached house* | calme/central | *central location* |
| mitoyenne | *semi-detached house* | près de... | *near to...* |
| attenante | *terraced house* | pratique pour... | *convenient for...* |
| l'Habitation à | | à la campagne | *rural situation* |
| Loyer Modéré | | | |
| (HLM) | *council flat / house* | la maison avec ... | *house with a ...* |
| la villa | *villa* | jardin | *garden* |
| le chalet | *chalet* | garage | *garage* |
| la ferme | *farm* | un garage pour | |
| l'auberge (f.) | *inn* | 2 voitures | *double garage* |
| | | une place | |
| l'agence immobilière | | de parking | *parking space* |
| (f.) | *estate agency* | le studio | *studio flat* |
| le crédit | | l'appartement | |
| immobilier | *mortgage* | (m.) | *flat* |
| l'expertise (f.) | *survey* | le trois-pièces | *two-bedroomed flat* |
| l'acheteur (m.) | *buyer* | | (two bedrooms and |
| le vendeur | *seller* | | a living room) |
| l'agent immobilier | | le duplex | *condominium,* |
| (m.) | *estate agent* | | *maisonette* |
| la clé | *key* | l'immeuble | |
| le prêt | *loan* | (m.) | *block of flats* |
| | | l'appartement | |
| la société de crédit | | loué | *rented flat* |
| immobilier | *building society* | la maison | |
| l'annonce (f.) | *advertisement* | louée | *rented house* |

| | | |
|---|---|---|
| Je suis | propriétaire(s) d'une | *I / we own our own house* |
| Nous sommes | maison | |

# 5  La maison et le jardin *Home and garden*

l'isolation (f.)    *insulation*
l'insonorisation
   (f.)    *sound proofing*
le double
   vitrage    *double glazing*
l'air conditionné
   (m.)    *air conditioning*
le chauffage
   central    *central heating*
le fioul    *oil*
le gaz    *gas*

le charbon    *coal*
l'électricité (f.)    *electricity*
le combustible
   solide    *solid fuel*
le bois    *wood*

acheter    *to buy*
louer    *to rent, to let*
emprunter    *to borrow*
payer    *to pay*

# 5 La maison et le jardin *Home and garden*

## LES PARTIES DE LA MAISON
### *PARTS OF THE HOUSE*

| | |
|---|---|
| la porte | *door* |
| l'allée (f.) | *drive* |
| la porte d'entrée | *front door* |
| le garage | *garage* |
| le portail | *gate* |
| le toit | *roof* |
| le mur | *wall* |
| la fenêtre | *window* |
| le grenier | *attic* |
| le balcon | *balcony* |
| le sous-sol | *basement* |
| la cave | *cellar* |
| l'escalier (m.) | *stairs* |
| la terrace | *terrace* |
| le rez-de-chaussée | *ground floor* |
| le premier étage | *first floor* |

## Les pièces  *Rooms*

| | |
|---|---|
| la salle de bains | *bathroom* |
| la chambre | *bedroom* |
| le débarras | *box room* |
| le coin repas | *dining area* |
| la salle à manger | *dining room* |
| l'entrée (f.) | *entrance hall* |
| la cuisine | *kitchen* |
| le palier | *landing* |
| le salon | *lounge* / *sitting room* |
| la salle de jeux | *play room* |
| la douche | *shower* |
| la chambre d'amis | *spare room* / *guest room* |
| le bureau | *study* |
| la buanderie | *utility room* |
| la véranda | *conservatory* |
| la bibliothèque | *library* |

## *ENCORE!*

● *Activity: Fill in the name of each room.*

# 5 La maison et le jardin *Home and garden*

## LES MEUBLES ET LA DÉCORATION
### *FURNITURE AND FURNISHINGS*

| | | | |
|---|---|---|---|
| le fauteuil | *armchair* | la prise | *plug* |
| le cendrier | *ashtray* | le radiateur | *radiator* |
| la baignoire | *bath* | la radio | *radio* |
| le lit | *bed* | le fauteuil | |
| la bibliothèque | *bookcase* | à bascule | *rocking chair* |
| la moquette | *carpet* | le tapis | *rug* |
| le magnétophone | *cassette recorder* | le drap | *sheet* |
| la chaise | *chair* | les étagères | |
| la commode | *chest of drawers* | (f.pl.) | *shelves* |
| l'horloge (f.) } | | l'évier (m.) | *sink* |
| la pendule } | *clock* | la prise | *plug* |
| la table basse | *coffee table* | la prise de | |
| la cuisinière | *cooker* | courant | *socket* |
| le lit d'enfant | *cot* | le canapé | *sofa / settee* |
| les rideaux (m.pl.) | *curtains* | le tabouret | *stool* |
| le coussin | *cushion* | l'interrupteur | |
| le lave-vaisselle | *dishwasher* | (m.) | *switch* |
| le placard | *fitted unit* | la table | *table* |
| le frigo | *fridge* | le téléviseur | |
| la chaise-haute | *high chair* | (m.) | *television set* |
| la plaque | | les tuiles (f.pl.) | *tiles* |
| chauffante | *hob* | les toilettes | |
| la lampe | *lamp* | (f.pl.) | *toilet* |
| le miroir | *mirror* | la serviette | *towel* |
| le four | *oven* | le magnétoscope | *video recorder* |
| l'oreiller (m.) | *pillow* | le placard | *wall cupboard* |
| le pot de fleur | *plant pot* | le papier peint | *wallpaper* |
| la couette { | *quilt* | la garde-robe | *wardrobe* |
| | *duvet* | le lavabo | *washbasin* |

---

## ENCORE!

● *Activity: What would you like ... for which room?*
I would like a _____ for the _____

J'aimerais _____ pour _____
Exemple: J'aimerais **un fauteuil** pour **le salon**

# 5 La maison et le jardin *Home and garden*

**LES TRAVAUX MÉNAGERS**
*HOUSEWORK*

| | |
|---|---|
| le produit WC | *toilet cleaner* |
| le papier toilette/ hygiénique | *toilet paper* |

Mon mari est homme au foyer.

| | |
|---|---|
| le produit nettoyant pour la salle de bain | *bathroom cleaner* |
| la brosse | *brush* |
| le seau | *bucket* |
| le balai mécanique | *carpet sweeper* |
| le shampooing pour moquettes | *carpet shampoo* |
| la shampooineuse | *carpet cleaner (machine)* |
| le chiffon | *cloth* |
| le détergent | *detergent* |
| le désinfectant | *disinfectant* |
| le chiffon à poussière } le plumeau | *duster* |
| la pelle | *dustpan* |
| le nettoyant pour les sols | *floor cleaner* |
| la cire | *furniture polish* |
| le sopalin | *kitchen towel roll* |
| le nettoyant pour le four | *oven cleaner* |
| la serpillère | *mop* |

| | |
|---|---|
| l'aspirateur (m.) | *vacuum cleaner* |
| le produit pour les vitres | *window cleaner (detergent)* |
| le laveur de carreaux | *window cleaner (man)* |
| la femme de ménage | *cleaner (woman)* |
| | |
| faire le ménage | *to do the cleaning* |
| faire la lessive | *to do the washing/ laundry* |
| nettoyer | *to clean* |
| faire les vitres | *to clean the windows* |
| épousseter | *to dust* |
| mettre la table | *to lay the table* |
| remplir le lave-vaisselle | *to load the dishwasher* |
| vider | *to unload* |
| faire les lits | *to make the beds* |
| faire briller } polir | *to polish* |
| passer l'aspirateur | *to vacuum* |
| faire la vaisselle | *to wash up* |
| essuyer | *to wipe* |

# 5 La maison et le jardin *Home and garden*

## LE JARDIN
### *GARDEN*

| | |
|---|---|
| l'horticulture (f.) | *horticulture* |
| le jardinage | *gardening* |
| le bulbe | *bulb* |
| le buisson | *bush* |
| le fertilisant | *fertiliser* |
| le parterre de fleurs | *flower bed* |
| les fleurs (f.pl.) | *flowers* |
| l'œillet (m.) | *carnation* |
| le chrysanthème | *chrysanthemum* |
| la marguerite | *daisy* |
| la rose | *rose* |
| l'herbe (f.) | *grass* |
| la serre | *greenhouse* |
| les herbes aromatiques (f.pl.) | *herbs* |
| la pelouse | *lawn* |
| le fumier | *manure* |
| l'allée (f.) | *path* |
| la plante | *plant* |
| le pot | *plant pot* |
| les graines (f.pl.) | *seeds* |
| l'arbuste (m.) | *shrub* |
| l'arbre (m.) | *tree* |
| le tronc | *trunk* |
| la branche | *branch* |
| la brindille | *twig* |
| la feuille | *leaf* |
| les arbres fruitiers (m.pl.) | *fruit trees* (See *Food and drink*, page 62) |
| les arbres en fleur (m.pl.) | *flowering trees* |
| le jardin potager | *vegetable garden* |

| | |
|---|---|
| les outils (m.pl.) | *tools* |
| la fourche | *fork* |
| le châssis | *frame* |
| la binette | *hoe* |
| le tuyau d'arrosage | *hose-pipe* |
| l'incubateur (m.) | *incubator* |
| la tondeuse à gazon | *lawn mower* |
| le rateau | *rake* |
| le sécateur | *secateurs* |
| la cisaille | *shears* |
| la bêche | *spade* |
| le déplantoir | *trowel* |
| l'arrosoir (m.) | *watering can* |
| la brouette | *wheel barrow* |

| | |
|---|---|
| la graine | *seed* |
| le semis | *seedling* |
| la plante | *plant* |
| la fleur | *flower* |
| la floraison | *blossom* |
| le fruit | *fruit* |
| les racines (f.pl.) | *roots* |

| | |
|---|---|
| creuser | *to dig* |
| couper l'herbe | *to cut the grass* |
| tondre la pelouse | *to mow the lawn* |
| planter | *to plant* |
| semer | *to sow* |
| tailler | *to prune* |
| arroser | *to water* |
| ramasser | *to gather* |
| désherber | *to weed* |
| fertiliser | *to fertilise* |
| cueillir | *to pick* |
| cultiver | *to cultivate* |
| faire pousser | *to grow* |

# 5 La maison et le jardin *Home and garden*

## LE MOBILIER DE JARDIN
### *GARDEN FURNITURE*

| | |
|---|---|
| le barbecue | *barbecue* |
| la vasque pour les oiseaux | *bird bath* |
| la mangeoire pour oiseaux | *bird table* |
| la cage à poules | *climbing frame* |
| la chaise longue | *deckchair* |
| la chaise de jardin | *garden chair* |
| la cabane | *garden shed* |
| le bassin | *paddling pool* |
| l'aire de jeu (f.) | *play area* |
| la cage à lapin | *rabbit hutch* |
| le manège | *roundabout* |
| le toboggan | *slide* |
| la balançoire | *swing* |
| le parasol | *sunshade* |

# 6 Les métiers et le travail *Jobs and work*

## LES MÉTIERS
### JOBS

| | |
|---|---|
| Je suis ... | *I am a / an ...* |
| comptable | *accountant* |
| acteur/actrice | *actor / actress* |
| agriculteur | *agricultural worker* |
| artiste | *artist* |
| boulanger (-ère) | *baker* |
| employé(e) | |
| de banque | *bank employee* |
| esthéticien(ne) | *beautician* |
| libraire | *bookkeeper* |
| maçon | *builder* |
| homme / femme | *businessman /* |
| d'affaires | *woman* |
| boucher (-ère) | *butcher* |
| acheteur (-euse) | *buyer* |
| poseur de | |
| moquette | *carpet fitter* |
| fonctionnaire | *civil servant* |
| employé(e) | |
| d'entretien | *cleaner* |
| employé(e) | |
| de bureau | *clerk* |
| directeur général | *company director* |
| informaticien(ne) | *computer operator* |
| programmeur | *computer* |
| (-euse) | *programmer* |
| cuisinier (-ière) | *cook* |
| coursier (-ière) | *courier* |
| dentiste | *dentist* |
| livreur / livreuse | *delivery man /* |
| | *woman* |
| docteur | *doctor* |
| chauffeur (-euse) | *driver* |
| electricien(ne) | *electrician* |
| ingénieur | *engineer* |
| fermier (-ière) | *farmer* |
| styliste | *fashion designer* |
| pompier | *fire fighter* |
| jardinier | *gardener* |

| | |
|---|---|
| dessinateur | |
| (-trice) | *graphic designer* |
| coiffeur (-euse) | *hairdresser* |
| dessinateur | *industrial* |
| industriel | *designer* |
| avocat(e) | *lawyer* |
| professeur | *lecturer, teacher* |
| bibliothécaire | *librarian* |
| chauffeur | |
| routier | *lorry driver* |
| P.D.G. (président- | |
| directeur | *managing* |
| géneral) | *director* |
| mécanicien | *mechanic* |
| infirmière | *nurse* |
| infirmier | *male nurse* |
| peintre- | *painter and* |
| décorateur | *decorator* |
| physiothérapeute | |
| kinésithérapeute } | *physiotherapist* |
| plombier | *plumber* |
| policier | *police officer* |
| facteur (-trice) | *postman* |
| agent des postes | *post office worker* |
| radiologue | *radiographer* |
| réceptionniste | *receptionist* |
| marin | *sailor* |
| vendeur | *salesman / woman;* |
| (-euse) | *shop assistant* |
| représentant(e) | *sales representative* |
| secrétaire | *secretary* |
| chanteur (-euse) | *singer* |
| soldat | *soldier* |
| notaire | *solicitor* |
| étudiant(e) | *student* |
| chirurgien(ne) | *surgeon* |
| chauffeur | |
| de taxi | *taxi driver* |
| enseignant(e) | *teacher* |
| téléphoniste | *telephonist* |
| serveur (-euse) | *waiter / waitress* |

# 6 Les métiers et le travail *Jobs and work*

*Note:*
To make the feminine form:
nouns ending **-ant** in the masculine: add an extra E
nouns ending **-eur** in the masculine: transform into -EUSE

| | |
|---|---|
| Je travaille ... | *I work ...* |
| à temps partiel } | |
| à mi-temps | *part-time* |
| à plein temps | *full-time* |
| en freelance | *freelance* |
| | |
| Je suis à mon compte | *I am self-employed* |
| Je suis au chômage | *I am unemployed* |
| | *out of work* |
| l'allocation de chômage (f.) | *unemployment benefit* |
| l'ANPE | *employment office* |
| (l'Agence Nationale pour l'Emploi ) | |
| la formation permanente | *re-training* |

## Les syndicats *Unions*

| | |
|---|---|
| le syndicat | *trade union* |
| les responsables syndicaux | *trades union officials* |
| le membre syndical | *trades union member* |
| la cotisation | *membership fee* |
| la carte de membre | *membership card* |
| la réunion syndicale | *trades union meeting* |
| le/la délégué(e) | *delegate* |
| le/la délégué(e) syndical(e) | *shop steward* |
| l'accord (m.) | *agreement* |
| la grève | *strike* |
| la grève du zèle | *work-to-rule* |

## Le salaire *Pay*

| | |
|---|---|
| les gains (m. pl.) | *earnings* |
| le salaire | *salary, wage* |
| le Smic | *minimum wage* |
| (Salaire minimum interprofessionnel de croissance) | |

| | |
|---|---|
| l'impôt sur le revenu (m.) | *income tax* |
| la Sécu | |
|   (la Sécurité sociale) | *National Insurance* |
| les cotisations retraite (f.pl.) | *pension contributions* |
| le jour de paie | *pay day* |
| l'enveloppe de paie (f.) | *pay packet* |
| la feuille de paie | *payslip* |
| le virement bancaire | *bank transfer* |
| les retenues (f.pl.) | |
| les prélèvements (m. pl.)   } | *deductions* |
| la TVA | |
|   (la Taxe sur la Valeur Ajoutée) | *VAT* |
| la retenue à la source | *PAYE* |
| chaque semaine | *weekly* |
| tous les mois | *monthly* |
| net | *net* |
| brut | *gross* |
| | |
| travailler | *to work* |
| gagner | *to earn* |
| faire un travail posté | *to work shifts* |
| faire des heures supplémentaires | *to do overtime* |
| aller en déplacement | *to travel* |
| avoir des réunions | *to have meetings* |
| vendre | *to sell* |
| acheter | *to buy* |
| pointer à l'arrivée | *to clock on* |
| pointer à la sortie | *to clock off* |
| être d'accord | *to agree* |
|      en désaccord | *to disagree* |
| discuter | *to discuss* |
| aller à une réunion | *to attend a meeting* |

## 6 Les métiers et le travail  *Jobs and work*

### AU TRAVAIL  *THE WORKPLACE*

| | |
|---|---|
| Je travaille . . . | *I work . . .* |
| Il/elle travaille dans . . . | *He / she works in a . . .* |
| | *on a . . .* |

| | | | | |
|---|---|---|---|---|
| une chaîne | | la production | *production* | |
| d'assemblage | *assembly line* | le contrôle de | | |
| les affaires (f. pl.) | | la qualité | *quality control* | |
| | *business* | un restaurant | *restaurant* | |
| une clinique | *clinic* | une boutique | *retail outlet, shop* | |
| un collège | *college* | la vente | *sales* | |
| une enterprise | *company* | la vente | | |
| un service | | en gros | *wholesale* | |
| après ventes | *customer service* | la vente | | |
| un service | | au détail | *retail* | |
| livraisons | *delivery* | une école | *school* | |
| l'équipement (m.) | | un magasin | *shop* | |
| | *equipment* | un studio | *studio* | |
| une usine | *factory* | une filiale | *subsidiary* | |
| un siège social | *head office* | un supermarché | | |
| un hôpital | *hospital* | | *supermarket* | |
| un hôtel | *hotel* | un cabinet | | |
| une société anonyme | | médical | *surgery* | |
| | *limited company* | un entrepôt | *warehouse* | |
| un bureau | *office* | un atelier | *workshop* | |
| l'emballage (m.) | *packaging* | à la maison | *at home* | |

---

### ENCORE!

● *Activity: Write a list of five jobs with their workplace.*

e.g. un mécanicien → un garage
Un mécanicien travaille dans un garage.

# 6 Les métiers et le travail   *Jobs and work*

## LA FABRICATION ET LES SERVICES
### *MANUFACTURING AND SERVICE INDUSTRIES*

Je travaille dans ...                     *I work in ...*
Je suis stagiaire dans ...                *I am a trainee in ...*
   l'industrie de fabrication (f.)      *the manufacturing industry*
   l'industrie des services (f.)       *the service industry*

| | |
|---|---|
| l'industrie (f.) | *industry* |
| l'agriculture (f.) | *agriculture* |
| l'horticulture (f.) | *horticulture* |
| l'industrie de l'acier | *the steel industry* |
| l'électronique (f.) | *the electronics industry* |
| la finance | *banking* |
| le commerce | *commerce* |
| l'industrie du tourisme | *travel and tourism* |
| l'industrie automobile | *the motor industry* |
| l'industrie minière | *the coal industry* |
| la recherche | *research* |
| la recherche scientifique | *science* |
| le génie électrique | *electrical engineering* |
| la constuction | *construction industry* |
| l'édition (f.) | *publishing* |
| la marine marchande | *shipping* |
| l'industrie médicale | *medical industry* |

| | |
|---|---|
| l'industrie phamaceutique | *pharmaceutical industry* |
| la restauration | *catering* |
| l'industrie alimentaire | *food industry* |
| la confection | *clothing* |
| la voirie | *road building* |
| le génie civil | *civil engineering* |
| la communication | *communications* |
| le design | *design* |
| l'industrie nucléaire | *nuclear power* |
| la mécanique industrielle | *machinery* |
| les transports (m. pl.) | *transport* |
| les télécommunications (f. pl.) | *telecommunications* |
| l'informatique (f.) | *information technology* |
| la fabrication de machines-outils | *tool machining* |
| le loisir | *leisure* |
| le tourisme | *tourism* |
| la vente | *sales* |

## 6 Les métiers et le travail   *Jobs and work*

| | |
|---|---|
| Je suis acheteur | *I am a buyer* |
| Je travaille avec des gens | *I work with people* |
| des machines | *machines* |
| des animaux | *animals* |
| des ordinateurs | *computers* |
| un tour | *a lathe* |
| le public | *the public* |
| du matériel informatisé | *computerised information* |
| Je dessine | *I design* |
| Je produis | *I manufacture* |
| Je vends | *I sell* |
| Je suis démonstrateur | *I demonstrate* |
| Je suis distributeur | *I distribute* |
| Je fais de la paperasserie | *I do the paperwork* |
| Je fais les comptes | *accounts* |
| Je fais le courrier | *I write letters* |
| Je suis publiciste | *I am in advertising* |
| Je co-ordonne | *I co-ordinate* |
| J'assiste | *I assist* |
| Je développe | *I develop* |

# 6 Les métiers et le travail *Jobs and work*

## LA CONSTRUCTION ET L'INDUSTRIE DU BÂTIMENT
### BUILDING AND THE CONSTRUCTION INDUSTRY

### Les travaux *Jobs*

| | |
|---|---|
| le maçon | *builder* |
| l'électricien (m.) | *electrician* |
| le chauffagiste | *heating engineer* |
| le menuisier | *joiner* |
| le laboureur | *labourer* |
| le peintre décorateur | *painter and decorator* |
| le plâtrier | *plasterer* |
| le plombier | *plumber* |
| le tailleur de pierres | *stonemason* |

### Les matériaux
*Building material and tools*

| | |
|---|---|
| la brique | *brick* |
| le ciment | *cement* |
| la bétonneuse | *cement mixer* |
| la construction | *construction* |
| l'embrasure de porte (f.) | *doorway* |
| le double vitrage | *double glazing* |
| les fondations (f. pl.) | *foundations* |
| le verre | *glass* |
| le gravier | *gravel* |
| l'isolation (f.) | *insulation* |
| l'échelle (f.) | *ladder* |
| la mesure | *measure* |
| le plâtre | *plaster* |
| le toit | *roof* |
| l'échaffaudage (m.) | *scaffolding* |
| les ardoises (f. pl.) | *slates* |
| la pierre | *stone* |

| | |
|---|---|
| la corde | *string* |
| les tuiles (f. pl.) | *tiles* |
| le bois | *timber, wood* |
| les murs (m. pl.) | *walls* |

### La plomberie *Plumbing*

| | |
|---|---|
| l'air climatisé (m.) | *air conditioning* |
| la chaudière | *boiler* |
| le chauffage | *heating* |
| les tuyaux (m. pl.) | *pipes* |
| les radiateurs (m. pl.) | *radiators* |
| le robinet | *tap* |
| le calorifuge | *lagging* |

### L'électricité *Electrics*

| | |
|---|---|
| l'ampère (m.) | *amp(s)* |
| le fusible | *fuse* |
| l'ampoule (f.) | *light bulb* |
| les luminaires (m. pl.) | *light fittings* |
| la prise | *plug* |
| l'interrupteur (m.) | *switch* |
| les volt | *volt* |
| les câbles électriques (m. pl.) | *wires* |

### La décoration intérieure
*Decorating*

| | |
|---|---|
| l'enduit (m.) | *filler* |
| l'échelle (f.) | *ladder* |
| la peinture | *paint* |
| le pinceau | *paint brush* |

# 6 Les métiers et le travail *Jobs and work*

| | |
|---|---|
| le décapant à peinture | *paint stripper* |
| la ponceuse | *sander* |
| le vernis | *varnish* |
| le papier peint | *wallpaper* |
| | |
| construire | *to build* |
| creuser | *to excavate* |
| marteler | *to hammer* |
| réparer | *to mend* |
| clouer | *to nail* |
| peindre | *to paint* |
| cimenter | *to plaster* |
| poncer | *to sand* |
| décoller/ décaper | *to strip (wallpaper / paint)* |
| construire | *to build* |
| faire les fondations | *to lay foundations* |
| réparer | *to repair* |

## Les outils *Tools*

| | |
|---|---|
| l'outillage (m.) | *tool kit* |
| la boîte à outils | *tool box* |
| la hâche | *axe* |
| le verrou | *bolt* |
| le câble | *cable* |

| | |
|---|---|
| le ciseau à bois | *carpentry chisel* |
| le burin | *stonemason's chisel* |
| le collier de serrage | *clamp* |
| la perceuse | *drill* |
| la perceuse électrique | *electric drill* |
| la rallonge électrique | *extension cable* |
| le marteau | *hammer* |
| le maillet | *mallet* |
| la clé anglaise | *monkey wrench* |
| le clou | *nail* |
| la pioche | *pick* |
| le rabot | *plane* |
| les tenailles (f. pl.) | *pliers* |
| la ponceuse | *sander* |
| la vis | *screw* |
| l'écrou (m.) | *nut* |
| le tournevis | *screwdriver* |
| la clé | *spanner* |
| l'établi (m.) | *workbench* |

| | |
|---|---|
| percer | *to drill* |
| marteler | *to hammer* |
| desserer | { *to undo* / *to loosen* } |

# 6 Les métiers et le travail *Jobs and work*

## LA SÉCURITÉ AU TRAVAIL *SAFETY AT WORK*

Port du casque obligatoire!!!
*Helmets must be worn at all times!!!*

| | |
|---|---|
| Ne pas toucher | *Do not touch* |
| utiliser | *use* |
| Danger! | *Danger!* |
| Attention! | *Warning!* |
| Entrée interdite | *No entry!* |
| Interdiction de fumer | *Smoking forbidden* |
| Accès interdit sauf personne autorisée | *No admittance except on business* |
| Porter des gants | *Wear gloves* |
| des lunettes de protection | *goggles* |
| un masque | *a mask* |
| des vêtements stériles | *sterilised clothing* |
| des vêtements de protection | *protective clothing* |
| Lavez-vous les mains | *Wash your hands* |
| Briser le verre! | *Break the glass!* |

| | | | |
|---|---|---|---|
| l'accident (m.) | *accident* | la trousse | |
| l'ambulance (f.) | *ambulance* | de secours | *medical kit* |
| la réanimation | *artificial* | la sortie | *exit* |
| | *resuscitation* | la sortie | *emergency exit,* |
| le choc | | de secours | *fire exit* |
| électrique | *electric shock* | le point de | *assembly point* |
| les services | | rassemblement | |
| d'urgence | *emergency* | l'extincteur (m.) | |
| (m. pl.) | *services* | | *fire extinguisher* |
| la chute | *fall* | l'alarme (f.) | *alarm* |
| les premiers secours | | les pompiers | |
| (m. pl.) | *first aid* | (m. pl.) | *fire brigade* |
| l'aide médicale | | le camion | |
| (f.) | *medical assistance* | de pompier | *fire engine* |

l'accident du
   travail (m.)   *industrial accident*
l'assurance (f.)   *insurance*

avoir un
   accident   *to have an accident*

se couper   *to cut oneself*
être électrocuté  *to be electrocuted*
tomber   *to fall*
avoir besoin   *to need emergency*
  de soins      *treatment*

# 7 L'entreprise *The company*

| | |
|---|---|
| le chambre de commerce | *chamber of commerce* |
| la société anonyme (SA) | *Limited company; Public Limited Company* |
| la société à responsabilités limitées (SARL) | *Limited liability company* |
| la société privée | *private business* |
| le service public | *public utility* |
| la politique de l'entreprise | *company policy* |
| la voiture de fonction | *company car* |
| le rapport d'entreprise | *company report* |
| la réunion d'entreprise | *company meeting* |
| la gestion | *management* |

| | |
|---|---|
| la conférence | *conference* |
| les atouts (m.pl.) | *assets* |
| le rachat | *buy-out* |
| l'offre de rachat (f.) | *take-over bid* |
| le marché | *deal* |
| le profit | *profit* |
| la perte | *loss* |
| la marge bénéficiaire | *profit margin* |
| les opérations (f.pl.) | *operations* |
| le développement | *development* |
| diriger | *to mange, to direct* |
| l'usine (f.) | *factory* |
| la firme l'entreprise (f.) } | *firm* |
| la franchise | *franchise* |
| l'agence (f.) | *agency* |

| | |
|---|---|
| le siège social | *head office* |
| la branche la succursale } | *branch* |
| la filiale | *subsidiary* |
| l'entrepôt (m.) | *warehouse* |
| les locaux (m.pl.) | *premises* |
| l'atelier (m.) | *workshop* |
| le magasin | *store* |
| les bureaux (m.pl.) | *offices* |
| non cloisonné | *open-plan* |
| la salle de conférences | *boardroom* |
| la réception | *reception* |
| le parking | *car park* |
| les toilettes (f.pl.) | *washrooms* |
| la cantine | *canteen* |
| le centre médical | *medical centre* |

# 7 L'entreprise *The company*

## LE PERSONNEL
### *THE WORKFORCE*

### Au bureau *In the office*

| | |
|---|---|
| le directeur { | *company director* / *manager* |
| le président- directeur général (P.D.G.) | *managing director* |
| le / la secrétaire de direction | *company secretary* |
| le directeur financier | *financial director* |
| l'assistant(e) | *personal assistant* |
| l'expert-conseil (m.) | *consultant* |
| le conseiller | *advisor* |
| l'adjoint (m.) | *deputy* |
| le conseil d'administration | *board of directors* |
| le cadre moyen | *middle management* |
| le contrôleur des crédits | *credit controller* |
| le directeur commercial | *commercial manager* |

| | |
|---|---|
| le patron | *boss* |
| le / la secrétaire | *secretary* |
| le / la réceptionniste | *receptionist* |
| la dactylo | *typist* |
| l'audiotypiste (m.f.) | *audio-typist* |
| la sténo-dactylo | *short-hand typist* |
| le / la documentaliste | *filing clerk* |
| le chef de bureau | *office supervisor* |
| le gardien | *security guard* |

| | |
|---|---|
| la standardiste | *switchboard operator* |
| le voyageur de commerce | *commercial traveller* |
| le / la représentant(e) | *representative* |
| le courtier en assurance | *insurance agent* |
| l'agent (m.) | *agent* |
| l'expert comptable (m.) | *auditor* |
| le courrier | *courier, mail* |
| l'ouvrier d'entretien (m.) | *cleaner* |
| en retraite | *retired* |
| la pension | *pension* |
| le / la pensionné(e), le / la retraité(e) | *pensioner* |

### Les ouvriers *The workers*

| | |
|---|---|
| l'apprenti(e) | *apprentice* |
| le gardien | *caretaker* |
| l'homme à tout faire | *handyman* |
| le contremaître | *overseer, foreman* |
| le chef d'équipe | *team leader* |
| le / la technicien (-ienne) | *technician* |
| le / la stagiaire | *trainee* |
| l'ouvrier (-ière) | *worker* |
| l'employeur (m.) | *employer* |
| l'employé(e) | *employee* |
| le laboureur | *labourer* |

| | |
|---|---|
| prendre sa retraite | *to retire* |
| renvoyer | *to sack* |
| licencier | *to make redundant* |

# 7 L'entreprise *The company*

| Je travaille dans le service ... | *I work in the ... department* |
|---|---|
| du personnel | *personnel* |
| des ventes | *sales* |
| du marketing | *marketing* |
| des achats | *buying* |
| de l'exportation | *export* |
| de l'importation | *import* |
| de la comptabilité | *accounts* |
| de la fabrication | *manufacturing* |
| de la qualité | *quality* |
| de la publicité | *publicity* |
| de l'administration | *administration* |
| technique | *technical* |
| des dactylos | *typing pool* |
|  |  |
| Je travaille par roulement | *I work shifts* |
| à plein temps | *full-time* |
| à mi-temps | *part-time* |
| J'ai des heures mobiles | *flexitime* |

# 7 L'entreprise *The company*

## LES VENTES, LA COMPTABILITÉ, LA DISTRIBUTION
### *SALES, ACCOUNTS AND DESPATCH*

### Les ventes *Sales*

| | |
|---|---|
| l'analyse (f.) | *analysis* |
| les affaires (f.pl.) | *business* |
| le voyage d'affaires | *business trip* |
| le concurrent | *competitor* |
| la plainte | *complaint* |
| le composant | *component* |
| l'ordinateur (m.) | *computer* |
| la réduction | *concession* |
| le consommateur | *consumer* |
| le contact | *contact* |
| la concession | *dealership* |
| la distribution | *distribution* |
| la documentation | *documentation* |
| franco de port | *franco (delivered 'free' with all duties paid)* |
| la garantie | *guarantee* |
| le marché intérieur | *home market* |
| extérieur | *export market* |
| l'offre (f.) | *offer* |
| la commande | *order* |
| les délais de paiement (m.pl) | *payment terms* |
| pour cent | *per cent* |
| le pourcentage | *percentage* |
| la performance | *performance* |
| l'achat (m.) | *purchase* |
| le devis | *quotation* |
| le détaillant | *retailer* |
| l'échantillon (m.) | *sample* |
| le dépositaire exclusif | *sole agency* |
| l'exclusivité (f.) | *exclusive rights* |
| le grossiste | *wholesaler* |
| la ristourne | *discount* |

| | |
|---|---|
| la vente par correspondance | *mail order* |

### La comptabilité *Accounts*

| | |
|---|---|
| le compte | *account* |
| le solde | *balance* |
| le code guichet | *bank code* |
| la faillite | *bankruptcy* |
| la facture | *bill* |
| comptant | *cash* |
| CAF (coût, assurance, fret) | *CIF (carriage, insurance and freight)* |
| la banque | *(clearing) bank* |
| la compensation | *compensation* |
| le coût | *cost* |
| le crédit | *credit* |
| les facilités de crédit | *credit facilities* |
| les conditions de crédit (f.pl.) | *credit terms* |
| le créancier | *creditor* |
| le délai | *deadline* |
| le débiteur | *debtor* |
| le bulletin de livraison | *delivery note* |
| la caution | *deposit* |
| sortie-usine | *ex-works* |
| la dépense | *expenditure* |
| l'expiration (f.) | *expiry* |
| les frais (m.pl.) | *fee, costs* |
| le dossier | *file* |
| la finance | *finance* |
| les prix fixes | *fixed costs / prices* |
| l'organigramme (m.) | *flow chart* |
| gratuit(e) | *free* |
| mon compte est créditeur | *I am in credit* |
| débiteur | *debt* |

# 7 L'entreprise *The company*

| | |
|---|---|
| la carte d'assurance | *insurance certificate* |
| la facture | *invoice* |
| la lettre de crédit | *letter of credit* |
| le paiement | *payment* |
| les délais de paiement | *payment terms* |
| la facture pro-forma | *pro-forma invoice* |
| la référence | *reference* |
| le règlement | *settlement* |
| le relevé | *statement* |
| le voucher | *voucher* |
| le déficit | *loss* |
| le reçu | *receipt* |
| le remboursement | *refund* |
| le numéro de référence | *reference number* |

## La distribution *Despatch*

| | |
|---|---|
| en stock | *available* |
| pas disponible | *not available* |
| le bon d'échange | *bill of exchange* |
| le bordereau de cargaison | *bill of lading* |
| l'arrivage (m.) | *consignment (incoming)* |
| l'envoi (m.) | *consignment (outgoing)* |

| | |
|---|---|
| le conteneur | *container* |
| la douane | *customs* |
| le retard | *delay* |
| le dépôt | *depot* |
| expédier | *to despatch* |
| l'équipement (m.) | *equipment* |
| excédentaire | *excess* |
| l'expédition (f.) | *forwarding* |
| le fret | *freight* |
| le transporteur | *freight forwarder* |
| les marchandises (f.pl.) | *goods* |
| entreposer | *to put in storage* |
| en stock | *in stock* |
| épuisé(e) | *out of stock* |
| le chargement | *load* |
| le réseau | *network* |
| le permis | *permit* |
| l'expédition par bateau | *shipment* |
| la taille | *size* |
| les frais de transport | *transport costs* |
| le poids | *weight* |
| le transport | *transport* |
| le transbordement | *transshipment* |
| le transit | *transit* |
| le document | *document* |
| valide | *valid* |
| périmé(e) | *out of date* |

# 7 L'entreprise *The company*

## LE MARKETING ET LA FABRICATION
### *MARKETING AND PRODUCTION*

| | |
|---|---|
| le commerce | *commerce* |
| le fabricant | *manufacturer* |
| le produit national brut | *gross national product* |
| les affaires (f.pl.) | *business* |
| le contrôle de commerce | *trade restrictions* |
| la barrière douanière | *trade barrier* |
| le tarif | *tariff* |
| l'interprète (m.f.) | *interpreter* |
| le quota | *quota* |
| la taxe à l'importation | *import duty* |
| à long terme | *long term* |
| à court terme | *short term* |
| le devis | *estimate* |
| la responsabilité | *liability* |
| la licence | *licence* |
| les négociations (f.pl.) | *negotiations, talks* |
| le négociateur | *negotiator* |
| officiel(le) | *official* |
| l'option (f.) | *option* |
| le paiement | *payment* |
| l'objectif (m.) | *target* |
| l'équipe de ventes (f.) | *sales team* |

| | |
|---|---|
| la marque | *trademark* |
| le logo | *logo* |
| le rendement | *output* |
| les matières premières (f.pl.) | *raw materials* |
| l'usine (f.) | *plant, factory* |
| la machinerie | *machinery* |
| la production de masse | *mass production* |
| le point de vente | *point of sale* |
| le progrès | *progress* |
| le projet | *project* |
| la promotion | *promotion* |
| la promotion des ventes | *sales promotion* |
| la campagne de vente | *sales campaign* |
| le budget | *budget* |
| la publicité | *publicity* |
| l'achat (m.) | *purchase* |
| la qualité | *quality* |
| le contrôle de qualité | *quality control* |
| la quantité | *quantity* |
| la gamme de produits | *range of goods* |
| le renouvellement | *renewal* |
| le rapport | *report* |

| | |
|---|---|
| l'étude de marché | *market research* |
| les tendances du marché (f.pl.) | *market trends* |
| le marketing | *marketing* |
| les prévisions du marché (f.pl.) | *market forecast* |
| être à la tête du marché | *to be the market leader* |

# 7 L'entreprise *The company*

| | | | |
|---|---|---|---|
| la recherche | *research* | le catalogue | *catalogue* |
| les termes | | la promotion | *promotion* |
| (m.pl.) | *terms* | la brochure | *brochure* |
| le programme | *schedule* | le poster | *poster* |
| le surplus | *surplus* | | |
| le transfert | *transfer* | vendre | *to sell* |
| la distribution | *distribution* | acheter | *to buy* |
| le contrat | *contract* | exporter | *to export* |
| le règlement | *regulations* | importer | *to import* |
| fait(e) main | *handmade* | livrer | *to deliver* |
| fabriqué(e) en | | transporter | *to transport* |
| série | *mass produced* | envoyer | *to send* |
| | | payer | *to pay* |
| la foire | | nommer | *to appoint* |
| exposition | *trade fair* | offrir une | |
| l'exposant (m.) | *exhibitor* | promotion | *to promote* |
| l'exposition (f.) | *exhibition* | sélectionner | *to select* |
| le stand | *stand* | | |

# 7 L'entreprise *The company*

## TRAVAILLER AU BUREAU
### WORKING IN THE OFFICE

## L'équipement *Equipment*

| | |
|---|---|
| Où est ...? | *Where is the ...?* |
| la calculatrice | *calculator* |
| le calendrier | *calendar* |
| la chaise | *chair* |
| la cafetière | *coffee machine* |
| l'ordinateur (m.) | *computer* |
| le bureau | *desk; office* |
| le dictaphone | *dictating machine* |
| le dictionnaire | *dictionary* |
| le tiroir | *drawer* |
| la punaise | *drawing pin* |
| l'enveloppe (f.) | *envelope* |
| le fax<br>le télécopieur } | *fax machine* |
| le dossier | *file* |

Je peux faire une photocopie? *Can I make a photocopy?*
Je peux utiliser le fax? *Can I use the fax machine?*
Tirer les stores/rideaux *To draw the blinds/curtains*
Ouvrir/fermer la fenêtre *To open/close the window*

| | |
|---|---|
| le classeur | *filing cabinet* |
| la machine à affranchir | *franking machine* |
| la colle | *glue* |
| le courrier reçu | *in-tray* |
| le courrier départ | *out-tray* |
| le papier | *paper* |
| le trombone | *paper clip* |
| le crayon | *pencil* |
| le téléphone | *phone* |
| le photocopieur | *photocopier* |
| l'imprimante (f.) | *printer* |
| le perforateur | *hole punch* |
| la gomme | *rubber/eraser* |
| la règle | *ruler* |

| | |
|---|---|
| les ciseaux (m.pl) | *scissors* |
| le scotch | *Sellotape* |
| la déchiqueteuse | *shredder* |
| les timbres (m.pl.) | *stamps* |
| l'agrafe (f.) | *staple* |
| l'agrafeuse (f.) | *stapler* |
| les étiquettes autocollantes (f.pl.) | *sticky labels* |
| le ruban adhésif | *sticky tape* |
| la table | *table* |
| l'effaceur (m.)<br>le Tipp-ex } | *Tipp-ex* |
| la machine à écrire | *typewriter* |
| le ventilateur | *ventilator* |
| la poubelle | *waste bin* |

## Se servir de l'ordinateur
### Using the computer

| | |
|---|---|
| le CD | *CD* |
| le curseur | *cursor* |
| la base de données | *database* |
| la disquette | *disquette* |
| le lecteur de disquette | *drive* |
| le courrier électronique | *electronic mail* |
| le disque dur | *hard disk* |
| l'icône (f.) | *icon* |
| la touche | *key* |
| le clavier | *keyboard* |

# 7 L'entreprise *The company*

| | |
|---|---|
| la marge | *margin* |
| la mémoire | *memory* |
| le modem | *modem* |
| la souris | *mouse* |
| la fiche | *plug* |
| l'imprimante (f.) | *printer* |
| le programme | *program* |
| la disquette | *soft disk* |
| le système son | *sound system* |
| le bouton marche-arrêt | *on / off switch* |
| la cassette | *tape* |
| l'ordinateur (m.) | *terminal* |
| le toner | *toner* |
| le window | *window* |

| | |
|---|---|
| le traitement de texte | *word processing* |
| le virus | *virus* |
| clicker | *to click* |
| rentrer | *to enter* |
| installer | *to install* |
| entrer | *to key in* |
| taper | *to press* |
| entrer dans le programme | *to get into the program* |
| recharger | *to re-fill* |
| sauver | *to save* |
| éteindre | *to switch off* |
| allumer | *to switch on* |
| taper | *to type* |
| souligner | *to underline* |

| | |
|---|---|
| Ça ne marche pas. | *It doesn't work.* |
| Comment tu ...? | *How do you ...?* |
| Comment tu l'allumes? | *How do you switch it on?* |
| Comment tu l'éteins? | *How do you switch it off?* |

# 8 Au téléphone *Using the telephone*

| | | | |
|---|---|---|---|
| le téléphone | *phone* | occupé | *engaged* |
| le standard | *switchboard* | le message | *message* |
| le poste | *extension* | en dérangement | *out of order* |
| le téléphone de | | le numéro de | |
| voiture | *car phone* | téléphone | *phone number* |
| l'Alphapage | | l'appel en P.C.V. | *reverse charges call* |
| (m.) | *pager* | le fax } | |
| le portable | *portable phone* | la télécopie } | *fax* |
| le modem | *modem* | téléphoner | *to phone* |
| le répondeur | *answering machine* | envoyer un fax | *to send a fax* |
| l'indicatif (m.) | *dialling code* | appeler | *to call* |
| la tonalité | *dialling tone* | rappeler | *to call back* |
| l'annuaire (m.) | *directory (enquiries)* | | |

| | |
|---|---|
| Allô! | *Hello!* |
| Vous désirez? | *Can I help you?* |
| Puis-je parler à ...? | *Can I speak to ...?* |
| Poste ... s'il vous plaît | *Can I have extension ...?* |
| Ne quittez pas! | *Hold on!* |
| Il/elle est absent(e). | *He/she is not there.* |
| Il/elle est en ligne. | *He/she is on the other line.* |
| Vous voulez qu'il/elle vous rappelle? | *Can I get him/her to call back?* |
| Vous voulez laisser un message? | *Can I take a message?* |
| Je vous remercie d'avoir appelé. | *Thank you for calling.* |
| Je vous en prie. | *Don't mention it.* |
| Désolé, j'ai fait un faux numéro. | *I'm sorry, I've got the wrong number.* |
| Vous pouvez rappeler? | *Can you call back?* |
| Épelez, s'il vous plaît. | *Can you spell it?* |
| Vous pouvez répéter, s'il vous plaît? | *Can you repeat it?* |
| Vous pouvez parler plus lentement, s'il vous plaît? | *Can you speak more slowly?* |
| Laissez un message après le bip sonore. | *Leave a message after the tone.* |
| Appelez après ... | *Ring after...* |

# 9 Les rendez-vous *Appointments*

## ARRANGER UN RENDEZ-VOUS ET S'EXCUSER
### *ARRANGING MEETINGS AND MAKING EXCUSES*

| | | | |
|---|---|---|---|
| On se retrouve où? | *Where shall we meet?* | au bar | *in the bar* |
| Rendez-vous ... | *Let's meet ...* | au parking | *in the car park* |
| à mon bureau | *in my office* | à l'hôtel | *in the hotel* |
| à ton / votre bureau | *at your office* | à la réception | *at reception* |
| chez moi | *at my house* | à l'arrêt de bus | *at the bus stop* |
| au restaurant | *at the restaurant* | à la gare | *at the station* |
| devant le cinéma | *in front of the cinema* | au carrefour de ... | *at the junction of ...* |
| dans le hall | *in the foyer* | sur le pont | *on the bridge* |
| au marché | *in the market place* | en face de la gare | *opposite the station* |
| | | sur le terrain de golf | *on the golf course* |

Je passe te prendre. — *I'll pick you up.*

On se retrouve à quelle heure? — *When shall we meet?*
Dans une demi-heure. — *In half an hour.*
Dans cinq minutes. — *In five minutes.*
Demain. — *Tomorrow.* (See also *The time*, page 16)

Je ne veux pas. — *I don't want to.*
Je ne peux pas. — *I can't.*
Je n'ai pas le temps. — *I haven't the time.*
J'ai trop de travail. — *I have too much work.*
Ça ne m'intéresse pas. — *I'm not interested.*
Je n'ai pas d'argent. — *I haven't any money.*
J'ai un rendez-vous. — *I have an appointment.*
Je suis occupé. — *I'm busy.*
Ma voiture n'a pas démarré. — *My car wouldn't start.*

Il faut que j'aille  chez le dentiste. — *I have to go to the dentist.*
                chez le docteur — *to the doctor*
                à l'hôpital — *to the hospital*

# 9 Les rendez-vous *Appointments*

## ENCORE!

● *Activity   What would you say?*

# 10 Les arts et les médias *Arts and the media*

## LES ARTS ET LES ARTISTES
### *ART AND ARTISTS*

| | |
|---|---|
| l'art (m.) | *art* |
| la galerie d'art | *art gallery* |
| la collection d'art | *art collection* |
| l'exposition (f.) | *exhibition* |
| l'artiste (m. f.) | *artist* |
| le dessinateur la dessinatrice le / la designer } | *designer* |
| le / la graphiste | *graphic artist* |
| l'illustrateur l'illustratrice } | *illustrator* |

## Le dessin et la peinture
### *Drawing and painting*

| | |
|---|---|
| la toile | *canvas* |
| le fusain | *charcoal* |
| les pastels (m. pl.) | *crayons* |
| le dessin | *drawing* |
| le croquis | *sketch* |
| la nature morte | *still life* |
| le chevalet | *easel* |
| le pinceau | *paint brush* |
| le tableau | *picture, painting* |
| le paysage | *landscape* |
| la peinture à l'huile | *oil painting* |
| le portrait | *portrait* |
| les couleurs (f. pl.) | *paints* |
| les pastels (m. pl.) | *pastels* |
| l'image (f.) | *picture* |
| le cadre | *picture frame* |
| l'aquarelle (f.) | *watercolour* |

## La poterie, la sculpture et l'architecture *Pottery, sculpture and architecture*

| | |
|---|---|
| le potier | *potter* |
| la poterie | *pottery* |
| la glaise | *clay* |
| le pot | *pot* |
| le tour | *wheel* |
| la sculpture | *sculpture* |
| le buste | *bust* |
| la gravure | *engraving* |
| le modèle | *model* |
| le ciseau | *sculptor's chisel* |
| le burin | *stonemason's chisel* |
| le studio | *studio* |
| le vernis | *varnish* |
| l'architecture (f.) | *architecture* |
| l'architecte (m.) | *architect* |
| le bâtiment | *building* |
| les plans (m. pl.) | *plans* |
| le style | *style* |
| romain(e) | *Roman* |
| classique | *Classic* |
| baroque | *Baroque* |
| gothique | *Gothic* |
| mouler | *to cast* |
| graver | *to carve, to engrave* |
| peindre | *to colour, to paint* |
| dessiner | *to design* |
| dessiner tracer } | *to draw* |
| sculpter | *to sculpt* |
| faire un croquis | *to sketch* |
| tourner | *to throw (clay)* |
| cuire faire chauffer } | *to fire* |
| vernir | *to varnish (a painting)* |
| vernisser | *to varnish (a pot)* |

# 10 Les arts et les médias *Arts and the media*

## LES LIVRES, LES MAGAZINES ET LES JOURNAUX
### BOOKS, MAGAZINES, NEWSPAPERS

| | |
|---|---|
| l'auteur (m.) | *author* |
| le biographe | *biographer* |
| l'écrivain (m.) | *writer* |
| le romancier | *novelist* |
| l'historien (-ienne) | *historian* |
| l'éditeur (-trice) | *publisher* |
| le poète | *poet* |
| le / la journaliste | *journalist* |
| le / la rédacteur (-trice) | *editor* |
| le / la photographe | *photographer* |
| le / la journaliste | *feature writer* |
| l'opérateur (-trice) informatique | *computer operator* |
| le concepteur | *designer* |
| le / la graphiste | *graphic designer* |

| | |
|---|---|
| la machine à écrire | *typewriter* |
| les droits d'auteur (m. pl.) | *royalties* |
| le traitement de texte | *word processing* |
| l'écriture (f.) | *handwriting* |

| | |
|---|---|
| le livre | *book* |
| le magazine | *magazine* |
| le quotidien | *daily* |
| l'hebdomadaire (m.) | *weekly* |
| le bi-hebdomadaire | *bi-weekly* |
| le mensuel | *monthly* |
| le journal | *newspaper* |

## Les livres *Books*

| | |
|---|---|
| la biographie | *biography* |
| la brochure | *brochure* |
| le roman policier | *crime story, detective story* |
| le dictionnaire | *dictionary* |
| l'autobiographie (f.) | *autobiography* |
| le document | *document* |
| l'encyclopédie (f.) | *encyclopaedia* |
| le livre de référence | *reference book* |
| le livre de poche | *paperback book* |
| le recueil d'expressions | *phrase book* |
| le livre de science-fiction | *sci-fi book* |
| la nouvelle | *short story* |
| le livre scolaire | *text book* |
| le roman à suspense<br>le polar | *thriller* |
| le guide de voyage | *travel book* |
| le conte de fée | *fairy tale* |
| la fiction | *fiction* |
| le guide | *guide book* |
| le roman historique | *historical novel* |
| la légende | *legend* |
| le manuel (d'utilisation) | *manual / handbook* |
| le roman | *novel* |
| la pièce | *play* |
| le poème | *poem* |
| la poésie | *poetry* |
| l'histoire (f.) | *story* |
| le volume | *volume* |

| | |
|---|---|
| le chapitre | *chapter* |
| le contenu | *contents* |

# 10 Les arts et les médias *Arts and the media*

| | |
|---|---|
| la couverture | *cover* |
| le livre relié | *hard cover* |
| le livre de poche | *paperback* |
| l'illustration (f.) | *illustration* |
| l'index (m.) | *index* |
| la ligne | *line* |
| la page | *page* |
| le papier | *paper* |
| le paragraphe | *paragraph* |
| l'expression (f.) | *phrase* |
| la phrase | *sentence* |
| le mot | *word* |
| | |
| écrire | *to write* |
| lire | *to read* |
| taper | *to type* |
| corriger | *to correct* |
| éditer | *to edit* |
| corriger les épreuves | *to proof-read* |
| publier en feuilleton | *to serialise* |
| imprimer | *to print* |

## La ponctuation *Punctation*

| | |
|---|---|
| la parenthèse | *bracket* |
| la virgule | *comma* |
| le point d'exclamation | *exclamation mark* |
| le point | *full stop* |
| le tiret | *hyphen* |
| les guillemets (m. pl.) | *inverted commas* |
| les accents (m. pl.) | *accents* |
| les fontes (f. pl.) | *founts* |
| les caractères (m. pl.) | *characters* |
| italique | *italic* |
| en caractères gras | *bold* |

| | |
|---|---|
| écrire en majuscules | *to use capital letters* |
| en minuscules | *small letters* |
| mettre en alinéa | *to indent* |
| ponctuer | *to punctuate* |

## La presse
### *Papers and magazines*

| | |
|---|---|
| les grandes lignes (f. pl.) | *outline* |
| le courrier du cœur | *problem page* |
| le feuilleton | *serial* |
| le titre | *headline* |
| la rubrique | *column* |
| la légende | *caption* |
| la mise en page | *layout* |
| la une | *front page* |
| l'éditorial (m.) | *editorial* |
| la publicité | *advertisement* |
| l'article (m.) | *article* |
| les petites annonces (f. pl.) | *small ads* |
| l'article de fond (m.) | *feature* |
| l'horoscope (m.) | *horoscope* |
| le courrier des lecteurs | *letters to the Editor* |
| les jeux (m. pl.) | *puzzles* |
| les BD (les bandes dessinées) | *cartoons* |
| la politique | *politics* |
| la société | *social* |
| le sport | *sport* |
| la revue | *review* |
| les nouvelles financières | *financial news* |
| internationales | *international news* |
| locales | *local news* |
| nationales | *national news* |
| boursières (f.pl.) | *stock market report* |
| la météo | *weather report* |

# 10 Les arts et les médias *Arts and the media*

## L'opinion *Opinion*

| | |
|---|---|
| l'enquête (f.) | *survey* |
| le questionnaire | *questionnaire* |
| l'avantage (m.) | *advantage* |
| le désavantage }<br>l'inconvénient } | *disadvantage* |
| il s'agit de ... | *it's a question of ...* |
| cela parle de ... | *it's about ...* |
| cela dépend | *it depends* |
| sans commentaire | *no comment* |
| selon les sondages | *according to the polls* |
| la différence | *difference* |
| la similarité | *similarity* |

| | |
|---|---|
| d'un côté | *on the one hand* |
| d'un autre côte | *on the other hand* |
| extraordinaire | *extraordinary* |
| habituel | *usual* |
| inhabituel | *unusual* |
| quand même | *all the same* |
| (en) bref | *in short* |
| pour conclure | *in conclusion* |
| finalement | *finally* |
| penser | *to think* |
| douter | *to doubt* |
| croire | *to believe* |
| avoir raison | *to be right* |
| avoir tort | *to be wrong* |
| préférer | *to prefer* |
| être nécessaire | *to be necessary* |

# 10 Les arts et les médias *Arts and the media*

## LE CINÉMA ET LE THÉÂTRE
### *CINEMA AND THEATRE*

### Le cinéma *The cinema*

| | |
|---|---|
| l'allée (f.) | *aisle* |
| l'audience (f.) | *audience* |
| le film | *film* |
| l'entrée (f.) | *foyer* |
| la séance | *showing* |
| le rang | *row* |
| l'écran (m.) | *screen* |
| le fauteuil | *seat* |
| la bande | *sound track* |
| (originale) | *(original)* |
| le ticket | *ticket* |
| le guichet | *ticket office* |
| la publicité | *advertisements* |

### Les genres de film
### *Film types*

| | |
|---|---|
| le film d'horreur | *horror film* |
| le western | *western* |
| le film policier | *detective thriller* |
| le film d'amour | *romance* |
| le film de | |
| science-fiction | *science fiction* |
| l'aventure de | |
| l'espace (f.) | *space adventure* |

| | |
|---|---|
| l'histoire | |
| d'amour (f.) | *love story* |
| porno | *pornographic* |
| censuré | *censored* |
| coupé | *cut* |
| interdit au moins de ... ans | |
| *not suitable for people under ... years* | |
| violent | *violent* |
| de guerre | *war* |

| | |
|---|---|
| la vedette | |
| de cinéma | *film star* |
| l'acteur | *actor* |
| l'actrice | *actress* |
| le réalisateur | |
| le metteur | } *director* |
| en scène | |
| le producteur | *producer* |
| l'assistant de | *production* |
| production | *assistant* |
| (m.) | |
| le caméraman | *cameraman* |
| l'ingénieur du | |
| son (m.) | *sound technician* |
| l'auditorium | |
| (m.) | *auditorium* |
| le balcon | { *balcony* / *circle* |
| la loge | *box* |

| | |
|---|---|
| C'était l'histoire de . . . | *It was about . . .* |
| C'était bien/passionnant/prenant/ bien tourné | *It was good / exciting / gripping / well filmed* |
| mauvais/affreux/ennuyeux | *bad / awful / boring* |
| C'était bien/mal filmé | *It was well / badly filmed* |
| Je (ne) le recommande (pas). | *I would (not) recommend it.* |

### Le théâtre *The theatre*

| | |
|---|---|
| Je voudrais deux billets pour . . . | *I would like two tickets for . . .* |
| C'est complet. | *It's sold out.* |
| Je voudrais réserver ... | *I would like to book ...* |

# 10  Les arts et les médias  *Arts and the media*

| | |
|---|---|
| l'auditorium (m.) | *auditorium* |
| le balcon | { *balcony* / *circle* |
| la loge | *box* |
| le vestiaire | *cloakroom* |
| le rideau | *curtain* |
| la sortie | *exit* |
| la sortie de secours | *emergency exit* |
| la rampe | *footlights* |
| l'orchestre (m.) | *front stalls* |
| le poulailler | *gallery* |
| les lumières (f. pl.) | *lights* |
| le décor | *scenery* |
| la scène | *stage* |
| les coulisses (f. pl.) | *wings* |
| | |
| acte 1 | *act 1* |
| l'acteur | *actor* |
| l'actrice | *actress* |
| les applaudissements (m. pl.) | *applause* |
| le personnage | *character* |
| le costume | *costume* |
| le critique | *critic* |
| la première | *first night* |
| l'entracte (m.) | *interval* |
| le texte | *lines* |
| le maquillage | *make-up* |
| la matinée | *matinee* |
| les nerfs (m. pl.) | *nerves* |
| le rôle | *part* |
| l'histoire (f.) | *plot* |
| la production | *production* |
| la séance | *performance* |
| le programme | *programme* |
| la répétition | *rehearsal* |
| le compte-rendu } la critique | *review* |

| | |
|---|---|
| la scène | *scene* |
| le décor | *set* |
| le spectacle | *show* |
| le trac | *stage fright* |
| | |
| l'opéra (m.) | *opera* |
| la distribution | *cast* |
| le soliste | *soloist* |
| le chœur | *chorus* |
| l'orchestre (m.) | *orchestra* |
| le chef d'orchestre | *conductor* |
| | |
| le ballet | *ballet* |
| le corps de ballet | *corps de ballet* |
| la danseuse étoile | *prima ballerina* |
| le danseur classique | *ballet dancer* |
| le danseur étoile | *principal* |
| le / la chorégraphe | *choreographer* |
| | |
| le drame | *drama* |
| le producteur | *producer* |
| le régisseur | *stage manager* |
| la doublure | *understudy* |
| l'acteur principal | *star* |
| le décorateur | *designer* |
| | |
| le cirque | *circus* |
| l'artiste (m.f.) | *artist* |
| le / la trapéziste | *trapeze artist* |
| l'acrobate (m.f.) | *acrobat* |
| le clown | *clown* |
| les animaux savants (m. pl.) | *performing animals* |
| la piste | *ring* |

# 10 Les arts et les médias *Arts and the media*

le spectacle de
  marionnettes *puppet show*
la comédie   *comedy*
la comédie
  musicale   *musical*
la revue   *revue*
la farce   *farce*
le drame
  historique   *historical drama*

jouer   *to act, to perform*
jouer le rôle
  de ...   *to play the role of ...*

danser   *to dance*
souffler   *to prompt*
tenir le rôle
  de ...   *to take the lead ...*
être figurant   *to have a*
    *walk-on part*

apprécier   *to enjoy*
regarder   *to watch*
(ne pas) aimer   *to (not) like*
huer   *to boo*
applaudir   *to clap, to applaud*

### LA MUSIQUE
### *MUSIC*

| | |
|---|---|
| le / la musicien (-ienne) | *musician* |
| le / la chanteur (-euse) | *singer* |
| l'instrument (m.) | *instrument* |
| le joueur | *player* |

| | |
|---|---|
| le groupe | { *band* / *group* } |
| les amplis (amplificateurs) (m. pl.) | *amplifiers* |
| les baffles (m. pl.) les haut-parleurs (m. pl.) | } *loudspeakers* |
| le D.J. | *disc jockey* |
| l'imprésario (m.) | *impresario* |
| le clavier | *keyboard* |
| la star | *pop / rock star* |
| la guitare | *guitar* |
| le / la guitariste | *guitarist* |
| la batterie | *drum kit* |

| | |
|---|---|
| le rock | *rock* |
| la pop | *pop* |
| la musique country and western | *country and western* |
| la musique folk | *folk* |
| le jazz | *jazz* |
| le rap | *rap* |

| | |
|---|---|
| la musique classique | *classical music* |

| | |
|---|---|
| le pianiste | *pianist* |
| l'accompagnateur (m.) | *accompanist* |
| l'orchestre (m.) | *orchestra* |

| | |
|---|---|
| le leader | *leader* |
| le chef d'orchestre | *conductor* |
| le soliste | *soloist* |
| le solo | *solo* |
| le duo | *duet* |
| l'orchestre de chambre (m.) | *chamber orchestra* |

| | |
|---|---|
| la partition | *score* |
| le compositeur | *composer* |
| la chorale le chœur | } *choir* |
| le soprano | *treble* |
| la soprano | *soprano* |
| le contralto | *alto* |
| le ténor | *tenor* |
| la basse | *bass* |

| | |
|---|---|
| les instruments à corde (m. pl.) | *strings* |
| le violon | *violin* |
| le violoncelle | *cello* |
| la viole | *viola* |
| la harpe | *harp* |
| la contrebasse | *double bass* |
| la guitare | *guitar* |
| le banjo | *banjo* |

| | |
|---|---|
| les instruments à vent (m. pl.) | *wind instruments* |
| la trompette | *trumpet* |
| le hautbois | *oboe* |
| la clarinette | *clarinet* |
| le saxophone | *saxophone* |
| le tuba | *tuba* |
| le trombone | *trombone* |
| le cor d'harmonie | *French horn* |
| la percussion | *percussion* |
| la batterie | *drums* |
| la cymbale | *kettle drum* |

# 10 Les arts et les médias *Arts and the media*

| | | | | |
|---|---|---|---|---|
| le tambour | *side drum* | | le bémol | *flat* |
| les castagnettes | | | le dièse | *sharp* |
| (f. pl.) | *castanets* | | le majeur | *major* |
| le tambourin | *tambourine* | | le mineur | *minor* |
| le triangle | *triangle* | | être accordé | *to be in tune (instrument)* |
| | | | chanter juste | *to be in tune (singer)* |
| le piano | *piano* | | | |
| l'accordéon (m.) | *accordeon* | | être désaccordé | *to be out of tune (instrument)* |
| le disque | *record* | | | |
| le tourne-disque | *record player* | | chanter faux | *to be out of tune (singer)* |
| la cassette | *cassette* | | | |
| le magnétophone | | | l'oreille absolue | |
| à cassettes | *cassette recorder* | | (f.) | *perfect pitch* |
| le disque compact | | | | |
| le CD | *CD* | | un bon/mauvais | *a good / poor* |
| le lecteur CD | *CD player* | | musicien | *musician* |
| le micro | *microphone* | | une bonne/mauvaise | |
| l'appareil | | | voix | *a good / poor voice* |
| enregistreur | | | | |
| (m.) | *recorder* | | jouer | *to play* |
| l'accord (m.) | *chord* | | accorder | *to tune* |
| l'air (m.) | *tune* | | chanter | *to sing* |
| la gamme | *the scale* | | tapoter du | |
| la clé | *key* | | piano | *to tinkle* |
| la | *A* | | gratter de la | |
| si | *B* | | guitare | *to strum* |
| do, ut | *C* | | graver un | |
| ré | *D* | | disque | *to cut a disk* |
| mi | *E* | | enregistrer { | *to record* |
| fa | *F* | | | *to tape* |
| sol | *G* | | | |

# 10 Les arts et les médias *Arts and the media*

## LA RADIO ET LA TÉLÉVISION
### *RADIO AND TELEVISION*

| | |
|---|---|
| la télé | *TV* |
| la radio | *radio* |

| | |
|---|---|
| le / la correspondant(e) | *correspondent* |
| la caméra vidéo | *video camera* |
| l'ingénieur du son (m.) | *sound engineer* |
| le caméraman | *cameraman* |
| l'enregistrement (m.) | *recording* |
| la bande annonce | *credits* |
| la chaîne | *channel* |
| l'interview (m.) | *interview* |
| les informations (f. pl.) | *news broadcast* |
| le magnétoscope | *video recorder* |
| l'interférence (f.) | *interference* |
| l'antenne (f.) | *aerial* |
| l'audience (f.) | *audience* |
| l'auditeur (-trice) | *listener* |
| le / la téléspectateur (-trice) | *viewer* |

| | |
|---|---|
| le / la présentateur (-trice) | *presenter* |
| le producteur | *producer* |
| l'éditeur (-trice) | *editor* |
| la télé commande | *remote control* |

| | |
|---|---|
| le programme | *programme* |
| le dessin animé | *cartoon* |
| la comédie | *comedy* |
| la publicité | *commercial* |
| le chat show | *chat show* |
| la rediffusion | *repeat* |
| les jeux télévisés (m. pl.) | *games show* |
| le feuilleton | *soap* |
| le documentaire | *documentary* |
| le documentaire touristique | *travel show* |

| | |
|---|---|
| allumer | *to switch on* |
| éteindre | *to switch off* |
| enregistrer | *to record* |
| repasser | *to play back* |
| régler | *to tune* |
| tomber en panne | *to break down* |
| effacer | *to wipe off* |
| changer de chaîne | *to change channels* |

| | |
|---|---|
| Tu as vu ...? | *Did you see ...?* |
| Comment tu as trouvé ...? | *What did you think of ...?* |

## LES PASSE-TEMPS
### *HOBBIES*

| | |
|---|---|
| le club | *club* |
| la danse | *dance* |
| la boîte de nuit | *night club* |
| le bar | *bar* |

| | |
|---|---|
| le bowling | *bowling alley* |
| la soirée | *party* |
| le casino | *casino* |
| le cirque | *circus* |
| la fête foraine | *fun fair* |
| le concert | *concert* |

| | |
|---|---|
| J'aime lire | *I like reading* |
| le jogging | *jogging* |
| danser | *dancing* |
| nager | *swimming* |
| jouer/écouter de la musique | *performing / listening to music* |
| me promener | *walking* |
| la randonnée | *hiking* |
| le jardinage | *gardening* |
| le bricolage | *D.I.Y.* |
| coudre | *sewing* |
| peindre | *painting* |
| dessiner | *drawing* |
| la photo | *photography* |
| les activités de plein air (f.pl.) | *outdoor pursuits* |
| tricoter | *knitting* |
| faire du vélo | *cycling* |
| faire du cheval | *horse riding* |
| pêcher | *fishing* |
| collectionner | *collecting* |
| les timbres (m.pl.) | *stamps* |
| les cartes postales (f.pl.) | *postcards* |
| les miniatures | *models* |
| sortir | *going out* |
| aller au cinéma | *going to the cinema* |
| au théâtre | *theatre* |
| au restaurant | *restaurant* |
| à la discothèque | *disco* |
| en boîte de nuit | *night club* |
| à une soirée | *party* |
| au gymnase | *sports centre* |
| J'aime jouer au tennis | *I like playing tennis* |
| J'aimerais jouer au tennis | *I would like to play tennis* |
| Je préfère aller boire un verre | *I prefer to go for a drink* |
| Je n'aime pas jouer au tennis | *I don't like playing tennis* |
| J'ai horreur de jouer au tennis | *I hate playing tennis* |

| | |
|---|---|
| le disco | *disco* |
| le champ de courses | *race course* |
| le parc | *park* |
| le parc d'attractions | *theme park* |
| le club de jeunes | *youth club* |
| la patinoire | *ice rink* |
| la piscine | *swimming pool* |
| le spectacle | *show* |
| le stade | *stadium* |

## Les jeux de cartes, les échecs et les jeux de société
### *Cards, chess and board games*

| | |
|---|---|
| le jeu de cartes | *pack of cards* |
| le cœur | *hearts* |
| le carreau | *diamonds* |
| le trèfle | *clubs* |
| le pique | *spades* |
| le roi | *king* |
| la reine | *queen* |
| le valet | *jack* |
| l'as (m.) | *ace* |
| le joker | *joker* |
| l'atout (m.) | *trump* |
| le whist | *whist* |
| le bridge | *bridge* |
| le joueur | *player* |
| jouer | *to play – to move* |
| À toi! } | *It's your turn!, It's your move!* |
| les échecs (m.pl.) | *chess* |

| | |
|---|---|
| la tour | *castle / rook* |
| le fou | *bishop* |
| le cavalier | *knight* |
| le pion | *pawn* |
| blanc | *white* |
| noir | *black* |
| roquer | *to castle* |
| échec au roi | *check* |
| échec et mat | *check mate* |
| Tu n'as pas le droit de faire cela! | *You can't do that!* |
| Tu dois ... | *You have to ...* |

| | |
|---|---|
| le jeu de société | *board game* |
| le dé | *dice* |
| le pion | *'man', piece* |
| la case | *'square'* |
| le sablier | *timer* |

## La danse *Dancing*

| | |
|---|---|
| le disco | *disco* |
| le tango | *tango* |
| la danse folklorique | *folk / country dancing* |
| la valse | *waltz* |
| la danse de salon | *ballroom dancing* |
| le swing | *jive* |
| le rock | *rock and roll* |
| le jazz | *jazz* |
| le pas | *step* |
| le/la partenaire | *partner* |
| le rythme | *rhythm* |
| la candence | *beat* |
| en mesure | *in time* |

### La pêche *Fishing*

Je suis parti à la pêche
*Gone fishing!*

| | |
|---|---|
| la pêche à la ligne | angling |
| le poisson | fish |
| l'eau de mer (f.) | salt water |
| l'eau douce (f.) | fresh water |
| la pêche à la mouche | fly fishing |
| la pêche à la ligne | coarse fishing |
| | |
| l'appât (m.) | bait |
| l'épuisette (f.) | basket |
| le bateau | boat |
| la mouche | fly |
| la mouche sèche | dry fly |
| le hameçon (m.) | hook |
| l'épuisette (f.) | landing net |
| la ligne | line |
| le filet | net |
| la rame | oar |
| la canne à pêche | rod |
| le tabouret | stool |
| les cuissardes (f.pl.) | waders |
| le plomb | weight |

| | |
|---|---|
| le poisson d'eau douce | freshwater fish |
| la truite | trout |
| la perche | perch |
| le saumon | salmon |
| le gardon | roach |
| | |
| le poisson d'eau de mer | sea fish |
| la morue | cod |
| le maquereau | mackerel |
| le hareng | herring |
| le thon | tuna |
| le poulpe | octopus |
| le requin | shark |
| l'encornet (m.) <br> la seiche | } squid |
| le merlan | whiting |
| | |
| les crustacés (m.pl.) | shellfish |
| le crabe | crab |
| le homard | lobster |
| la crevette | shrimp |
| la crevette rose | prawn |
| la langoustine | langoustine |
| les moules (f.pl.) | mussels |
| les coques (f.pl.) | cockles |
| les coquilles Saint-Jacques (f.pl.) | scallops |
| | |
| pêcher | to fish |
| attraper | to catch |

Il était grand comme ça!

# 11 Les passe-temps et les sports *Hobbies and sports*

## Les chevaux et l'équitation
### *Horses and riding*

| | |
|---|---|
| le poney | *pony* |
| le cheval | *horse* |
| la jument | *mare* |
| l'étalon (m.) | *stallion* |
| la selle | *saddle* |
| la bride | *bridle* |
| le harnais | *harness* |
| l'écurie (f.) | *stable* |
| le paddock | *paddock* |
| le saut | *jump* |
| la veste d'équitation | *riding coat* |
| les jodhpurs | *jodhpurs* |
| la bombe | *riding hat* |
| la cravache | *crop* |
| les bottes d'équitation (f.pl.) | *riding boots* |
| le cheval de courses (m.pl.) | *race-horse* |
| l'hippodrome (m.) | *race course* |
| le vainqueur | *winner* |
| la pari | *bet* |
| le jockey | *jockey* |
| la course de plat | *flat race* |
| le bookmaker | *bookie* |

| | |
|---|---|
| parier | *to bet* |
| tomber de... | *to fall off* |
| panser | *to groom* |
| sauter | *to jump* |
| monter à cheval | *to horse-ride* |
| aller au trot | *to trot* |
| gagner | *to win* |

## La photographie
### *Photography*

| | |
|---|---|
| le/le photographe | *photographer* |
| l'album (m.) | *album* |

| | |
|---|---|
| l'ouverture (f.) | *aperture* |
| automatique | *automatic* |
| la pile | *battery* |
| noir et blanc | *black and white* |
| l'appareil photo (m.) | *camera* |
| la couleur | *colour* |
| la chambre noire | *dark room* |
| l'agrandissement (m.) | *enlargement* |
| le photomètre | *exposure meter* |
| la pellicule | *film* |
| la pellicule rapide | *fast film* |
| le flash | *flash* |
| l'ampoule de flash (f.) | *flash bulb* |
| l'objectif (m.) | *lens* |
| le bouchon d'objectif | *lens cap* |
| le photomètre | *light meter* |
| mat/brillant | *matt / glossy* |
| le négatif | *negative* |
| la photo | *print* |
| le réglage | *setting* |
| le téléobjectif | *telephoto lens* |
| le retardateur | *timing* |
| la diapositive | *transparency* |
| le trépied | *tripod* |
| sous exposé | *under exposed* |
| viseur | *view finder* |
| grand angle | *wide angle* |
| le flash ne marche pas | *the flash doesn't work* |

| | |
|---|---|
| développer | *to develop* |
| agrandir | *to enlarge* |
| exposer | *to expose* |
| régler | *to focus* |
| tirer | *to print* |
| rembobiner | *to re-wind* |
| prendre une photo | *to take a photo* |

110

## LES SPORTS
### SPORTS – GENERAL

| | |
|---|---|
| le foot | *football* |
| le rugby | *rugby* |
| le ballon | *ball* |
| le badminton | *badminton* |
| le volant | *badminton feather* |
| le filet | *net* |
| la raquette | *racquet* |
| le squash | *squash* |
| le court | *court* |
| le netball | *netball* |
| le handball | *handball* |
| le volleyball | *volleyball* |
| le basketball | *basketball* |
| | |
| la planche à roulettes | *skate boarding* |
| la rampe | *ramp* |
| le patin à roulettes | *roller skating* |
| | |
| le ping pong | *table tennis* |
| la table de ping pong | *table tennis table* |
| la raquette | *bat* |
| l'escrime (f.) | *fencing* |
| le masque | *mask* |
| le fleuret | *foil* |
| | |
| le tir à l'arc | *archery* |
| l'arc (m.) | *bow* |
| la flèche | *arrow* |
| la cible | *target* |
| | |
| la boxe | *boxing* |
| le ring | *ring* |
| les gants (m.pl.) | *gloves* |
| la lutte ⎱ le catch ⎰ | *wrestling* |
| | |
| le tir | *shooting* |

| | |
|---|---|
| le fusil | *rifle* |
| la cible | *rifle range* |
| les munitions (f.pl.) | *ammunition* |
| la balle | *bullet* |
| le tir au pigeon ⎱ la ball-trap ⎰ | *clay pigeon shooting* |
| | |
| le billard | *billiards* |
| le jeu de billard | *snooker* |
| le billard américain | *pool* |
| la queue de billard | *cue* |
| la boule | *billiard ball* |
| la table de billard | *billiard table* |
| | |
| les fléchettes (f.pl.) | *darts* |
| la cible | *dart board* |
| | |
| les boules (f.pl.) | *bowls* |
| le cochonnet | *jack* |
| le jeu de quilles | *skittles* |
| | |
| la gymnastique | *gymnastics* |
| le trampoline | *trampoline* |
| les barres parallèles (f.pl) | *parallel bars* |
| le tapis | *mat* |
| le cheval-arçons | *vaulting horse* |
| le sol | *floor* |
| | |
| le hockey | *hockey* |
| la canne | *stick* |
| la cage | *goal* |
| | |
| la musculation | *fitness training* |
| les poids (m.pl.) | *weights* |
| l'aérobic (f.) | *aerobics* |
| cardiovasculaire | *cardiovascular* |

| | |
|---|---|
| le jogging | *jogging* |
| le vélo | |
| d'appartement | *exercise bike* |

| | |
|---|---|
| l'équipement de protection (m.) | *protective equipment* |
| la garde | *guard* |
| le bouclier | *shields* |

| | |
|---|---|
| les arts martiaux (m.pl.) | *martial arts* |
| le judo | *judo* |
| le tae kwando | *tae kwando* |
| la tenue | *suit* |
| la ceinture | *belt* |

| | |
|---|---|
| le juge | *judge* |
| le chronométreur | *time keeper* |
| le chronomètre | *stopwatch* |
| le tour | *lap* |
| le pistolet de starter | *starting gun* |

| | |
|---|---|
| les sports aériens (m.pl.) | *air sports* |
| le parachutisme | *parachuting* |
| l'U.L.M. (ultra léger motorisé) | *gliding* |
| le parapente | *paragliding* |
| le delta-plane | *hang gliding* |

| | |
|---|---|
| l'aviation (f.) | *flying* |
| l'ascension en ballon (f.) | *ballooning* |

| | |
|---|---|
| les sports alpins (m.pl) | *mountain sports* |
| l'alpinisme (m.) | *climbing* |
| la varappe l'escalade (f.) | *rock climbing* |
| l'exercice d'orientation (m.) | *orienteering* |
| la corde | *rope* |
| les chaussures de montagne (f.pl.) | *climbing boots* |
| la voie | *route* |
| le harnais (m.) | *harness* |
| faire de la randonnée en montagne | *mountain walking / hiking* |
| le piolet | *ice axe* |
| le sac à dos | *rucksack* |
| les vêtements thermolactyl (m.pl.) | *thermal clothing* |
| les pitons (m.pl.) | *pitons* |

| | |
|---|---|
| les sports nautiques (m.pl.) | *water sports* |
| les sports d'hiver (m.pl) | *winter sports* |

## LES SPORTS EN DÉTAIL
### *SPORTS IN DETAIL*

### Le foot  *Football*

| | |
|---|---|
| l'équipe (f.) | *team* |
| le match | *match* |
| le club | *club* |
| le terrain de foot | *pitch* |
| | |
| l'arbitre (m.) | *referee* |
| le juge de touche | *linesman* |
| le gardien de stade | *groundsman* |
| le/la spectateur (-trice) | *spectator* |
| le joueur | *player* |
| le capitaine | *captain* |
| le directeur du club | *team manager* |
| | |
| la ligue | *league* |
| la compétition | *competition* |
| la coupe | *cup* |
| | |
| le but | *goal* |
| la touche | *line* |
| le poteau de but | *goal post* |
| hors jeu | *off-side* |
| | |
| les positions (f.pl.) | *positions* |
| le gardien de but | *goalkeeper* |
| l'attaque (f.) | *attack* |
| la défense | *defence* |
| le centre | *centre* |
| l'arrière (m.) | *back* |
| l'avant (m.) | *forward* |
| | |
| gagner | *to win* |

| | |
|---|---|
| faire match nul | *to draw* |
| perdre | *to lose* |
| marquer un but | *to score* |
| taper dans le ballon | *to kick* |
| rater | *to miss* |

### Le tennis  *tennis*

| | |
|---|---|
| le match | *match* |
| simple | *singles* |
| double | *doubles* |
| le/la partenaire | *partner* |
| l'adversaire (m.f.) | *opponent* |
| | |
| la raquette | *racquet* |
| la balle | *ball* |
| le filet | *net* |
| la ligne | *line* |
| le service | *service* |
| le set<br>la manche } | *set* |
| zéro | *love* |
| jeu, set et match | *game, set and match* |
| le let | *let* |
| égalité | *deuce* |
| | |
| servir | *to serve* |
| jouer | *to play* |
| reprendre de volée | *to volley* |

### Le golf  *Golf*

| | |
|---|---|
| le terrain de golfe | *golf course* |
| le trou | *hole* |
| le drapeau | *flag* |
| le bunker | *bunker* |
| le green | *green* |

# 11 Les passe-temps et les sports *Hobbies and sports*

le club  
la crosse } *club*

le fer — *iron*
le bois — *wood*
le putter — *putter*
la balle — *ball*
le tee — *tee*

putter — *to putt*
driver — *to drive*
cocher — *to chip*

## Le cyclisme *Cycling*

le vélo de
  compétition — *racing bike*
les roues (f.pl.) — *wheels*
la pompe — *pump*
le guidon — *handlebars*
les freins (m.pl.) — *brakes*
la chaîne — *chain*
le pneu crevé — *puncture*
les pédales
  (f.pl.) — *pedals*
la selle — *saddle*
les rayons
  (m.pl.) — *spokes*
la chambre à air
  de rechange — *spare inner tube*
le short de
  cyclisme — *cycling shorts*
le maillot — *shirt*
le casque — *helmet*
les gants (m.pl.) — *gloves*
les chaussures
  (f.pl.) — *shoes*
le VTT — *mountain bike*
  (vélo tout terrain)

## L'athlétisme *Athletics*

le stade — *stadium*
la piste — *track*
la course de
  haies — *hurdles*
les starting
  blocks (m.pl) — *blocks*
les officiels
  (m.pl.) — *officials*
le chronométreur
  — *timekeeper*
les participants
  (m.pl) — *competitors*
le concours — *field event*
l'épreuve
  sur piste (f.) — *track event*

courir — *to run*
marcher — *to walk*

le marathon — *marathon*
le saut — *jump*
le saut en
  longueur — *long jump*
le saut en
  hauteur — *high jump*
le saut à
  la perche — *pole valut*
le triple saut — *triple jump*
le biathlon — *biathlon*
le marathon — *marathon*
la course
  de relais — *relay race*
le cross — *cross country*
le lancer
  du poids — *putting the shot*
  du marteau — *throwing the hammer*
  du javelot — *throwing the javelin*

114

# 11 Les passe-temps et les sports *Hobbies and sports*

## Les sports nautiques
### *Water sports*

| | |
|---|---|
| la natation | *swimming* |
| la brasse | *breast stroke* |
| le crawl | *crawl* |
| la nage libre | *free style* |
| le dos crawlé | *back stroke* |
| le papillon | *butterfly* |
| la longueur | *length* |
| le relais | *relay* |
| la nage de vitesse | *speed stroke* |
| le maillot de bain | *swimming costume* |
| le bonnet de bain | *swimming hat* |
| les lunettes de piscine (f.pl.) | *goggles* |
| les palmes (f.pl.) | *flippers* |
| le tuba | *snorkel* |
| la lotion solaire (qui résiste à l'eau) | *(water resistant) sun cream* |
| la plongée | *diving* |
| le plongeoir | *diving board* |
| faire un plat | *to do a belly flop* |
| plonger | *to dive* |
| la plongée sous-marine | *underwater diving* |
| la combinaison de plongée | *wet suit* |
| la bouteille d'oxygène | *oxygen cylinder* |
| le canyoning | *canyoning* |
| le radeau | *rafting* |
| l'aviron (.m) | *rowing* |
| le canoë | *canoeing* |
| le kayak | *kayak* |
| la pagaie | *paddle* |
| le gilet de sauvetage | *life jacket* |

| | |
|---|---|
| la barque | *rowing boat* |
| les rames (f.pl.) | *oars* |
| la barre | *helm* |
| la poupe | *stern* |
| la voile | *sailing* |
| la bateau | *boat* |
| le canot pneumatique | *dinghy* |
| la voile | *sail* |
| le gouvernail | *rudder* |
| la barre de gouvernail | *tiller* |
| le cordage | *rope* |
| l'écoute de la grand voile (f.) | *main sheet* |
| le tribord | *starboard* |
| le port | *port* |
| les espars (m.pl.) | *spars* |
| la quille | *keel* |
| la dérive | *centreboard* |
| chavirer | *to capsize* |
| le ski nautique | *water skiing* |
| le bateau à moteur | *motor boat* |
| le hors-bord | *outboard (motor)* |

## Les sports d'hiver
### *Winter sports*

| | |
|---|---|
| le ski | *skiing* |
| le ski alpin | *alpine skiing* |
| le ski de fond | *cross-country skiing* |
| les skis (m.pl.) | *skis* |
| les bâtons (m.pl.) | *ski poles* |
| les chaussures de ski (f.pl.) | *ski boots* |
| la piste | *piste* |

| | |
|---|---|
| le remonte-pente | *ski lift* |
| le forfait | *ski pass* |
| la station de sports d'hiver | *ski resort* |
| la salopette | *salopette* |
| le slalom | *slalom* |
| la descente | *downhill race* |
| le saut à ski | *ski jumping* |
| le surf des neiges | *snowboarding* |
| un surf | *board* |
| les fixations (f.pl) | *bindings* |
| les chaussures (f.pl.) | *boots* |
| figures libres | *free style* |

| | |
|---|---|
| le toboggan | *toboggan* |
| la piste de toboggan | *toboggan run* |
| le patin à glace | *ice skating* |
| les patins (m.pl.) | *skates* |
| le patinage artistique | *ice dance* |
| la patinoire | *skating rink* |
| le hockey sur glace | *ice hockey* |
| le palet | *puck* |
| la crosse de hockey | *hockey stick* |
| le but | *goal* |

# 12 Le corps et la santé *The body and health*

## LE CORPS
### *THE BODY*

### Les parties du corps
#### *Parts of the body*

| | |
|---|---|
| le corps | *body* |
| le visage | *face* |
| le tête | *head* |
| la gorge | *throat* |
| le cou | *neck* |
| l'épaule | *shoulder* |
| le bras | *arm* |
| le coude | *elbow* |
| le poignet | *wrist* |
| le poing | *fist* |
| la main | *hand* |
| le doigt | *finger* |
| le pouce | *thumb* |
| l'annulaire (m.) | *ring finger* |
| l'auriculaire (m.) | *little finger* |
| l'index (m.) | *index finger* |
| l'ongle (m.) | *fingernail* |
| la poitrine | *chest* |
| le buste | *bust* |
| les côtes (f. pl.) | *ribs* |
| le devant | *front* |
| le côté | *side* |
| le dos | *back* |
| la taille | *waist* |
| les hanches (f. pl.) | *hips* |
| | |
| la jambe | *leg* |
| la cuisse | *thigh* |
| le genou | *knee* |
| le mollet | *calf* |
| la cheville | *ankle* |
| le pied | *foot* |
| le talon | *heel* |
| la plante des pieds | *sole* |
| le doigt de pied | *toe* |

| | |
|---|---|
| la peau | *skin* |
| l'os (m.) | *bone* |
| l'articulation (f.) | *joint* |
| la colonne vertébrale | *spine* |
| le squelette | *skeleton* |
| le crâne | *skull* |

### Les organes internes
#### *Internal organs*

| | |
|---|---|
| le cerveau | *brain* |
| le cœur | *heart* |
| le sang | *blood* |
| le vaisseau sanguin | *blood vessel* |
| l'artère (f.) | *artery* |
| la veine | *vein* |
| le pouls | *pulse* |
| les intestins (m. pl.) | *intestines* |
| les reins (m. pl.) | *kidneys* |
| le foie | *liver* |
| les poumons (m. pl.) | *lungs* |
| les nerfs (m. pl.) | *nerves* |
| l'estomac (m.) | *stomach* |
| le vagin | *vagina* |
| l'utérus (m.) | *womb* |
| le col de l'utérus | *cervix* |
| le pénis | *penis* |

# 12 Le corps et la santé *The body and health*

| | | | |
|---|---|---|---|
| la prostate | *prostate (gland)* | faire du jogging | *to jog* |
| le ligament | *ligament* | sauter | *to jump* |
| le muscle | *muscle* | s'agenouiller | *to kneel* |
| le système | | s'allonger | *to lie down* |
|   nerveux | *nervous system* | se reposer | *to rest* |
| le tendon | *tendon* | courir | *to run* |
| | | s'asseoir | *to sit* |
| respirer | *to breathe* | dormir | *to sleep* |
| faire de | | se tenir debout | *to stand* |
|   l'exercice | *to exercise* | marcher | *to walk* |

## Les douleurs
### *Aches and pains*

| | |
|---|---|
| Ça fait mal. | *It hurts.* |
| J'ai mal au dos | *I've got (a) backache* |
|   mal aux oreilles | *earache* |
|   mal à la tête | *headache* |
|   mal aux dents | *toothache* |
|   mal au doigt | *sore finger* |
|   une ampoule | *blister* |

## Le visage *The face*

| | | | |
|---|---|---|---|
| le visage | *face* | la rétine | *retina* |
| la peau | *complexion* | les sourcils (m. pl.) | |
| les joues (f. pl.) | *cheeks* | | *eyebrows* |
| le menton | *chin* | les cils (m. pl.) | *eyelashes* |
| l'oreille (f.) | *ear* | la paupière | *eyelid* |
| l'œil (m.) | *eye* | le front | *forehead* |
| | | les cheveux (m. pl.) | |
| | | | *hair* |
| | | les lèvres (f. pl.) | *lips* |
| | | la bouche | *mouth* |
| | | le nez | *nose* |
| | | la peau | *skin* |
| | | les dents (f. pl.) | *teeth* |
| l'iris (m.) | *iris* | la langue | *tongue* |
| le cristallin | *lens* | | |

| | |
|---|---|
| J'ai un (des) bouton(s) | *I've got a spot / spots* |
| un furoncle | *a boil* |
| un point noir | *a blackhead* |
| une oreille bouchée | *a blocked ear* |
| du cérumen | *ear wax* |
| un nez bouché | *a stuffed nose* |
| le rhume chronique $\Big\}$ | *catarrh* |
| un catarrhe | |
| des pellicules (f. pl.) | *dandruff* |

| | | | | |
|---|---|---|---|---|
| sourire | *to smile* | éternuer | *to sneeze* |
| froncer les | | tousser | *to cough* |
| sourcils | *to frown* | | |
| faire la grimace | *to grimace, to make a face* | | |

# 12 Le corps et la santé *The body and health*

## LE NÉCESSAIRE DE TOILETTE ET LES COSMÉTIQUES
### *TOILETRIES AND COSMETICS*

| Avez vous ...? | *Have you got a / some ...?* |
|---|---|
| de l'après rasage | *aftershave* |
| un peigne | *comb* |
| de l'après shampooing | *conditioner* |
| des préservatifs (m. pl.) | *condoms* |
| du fil dentaire | *dental floss* |
| du déodorant | *deodorant* |
| un gant de toilette | *face cloth* |
| de la crème pour le visage | *face cream* |
| un masque de beauté | *face pack* |
| une brosse à cheveux | *hairbrush* |
| un sèche cheveux | *hair dryer* |
| de la cire à épiler | *leg wax* |
| de la crème adoucissante | *moisturiser* |
| un bain de bouche ⎫<br>un élixir dentaire ⎭ | *mouth wash* |
| une lime à ongles | *nail file* |
| des ciseaux à ongles | *nail scissors* |
| du vernis à ongles (m. pl.) | *nail varnish* |
| du dissolvant | *nail varnish remover* |
| un mouchoir en papier | *paper handkerchief* |
| un rasoir | *razor* |
| des rasoirs jetables (m. pl.) | *disposable razors* |
| un rasoir électrique | *electric razor* |
| des serviettes hygiéniques (f. pl.) | *sanitary towels* |
| du shampooing | *shampoo* |
| un blaireau | *shaving brush* |
| de la mousse à raser | *shaving cream* |
| du savon | *soap* |
| une éponge | *sponge* |
| une trousse de toilette | *sponge bag* |
| de la crème solaire | *sun cream* |
| après soleil | *after-sun cream* |
| du talc | *talcum powder* |
| un tampon | *tampon* |
| une brosse à dents | *toothbrush* |
| du dentifrice | *toothpaste* |
| une pince à épiler | *tweezers* |

# 12 Le corps et la santé *The body and health*

Je voudrais quelque chose pour (les boutons). *I need something for (spots).*

| | | | |
|---|---|---|---|
| se laver | *to wash* | le blush | *blusher* |
| se brosser | *to brush* | le pinceau à blush | *make-up brush* |
| nettoyer | *to clean* | l'ombre à | |
| utiliser | *to use* | paupières (f.) | *eye shadow* |
| mettre | *to put on* | l'eye-liner (m.) | *eye liner* |
| | | la poudre | *face powder* |
| se mettre du vernis | | le mascara | *mascara* |
| à ongles | *to varnish one's nails* | le rouge à lèvres | *lipstick* |
| enlever du vernis | | | |
| à ongles | *to remove varnish* | se laver les cheveux | *to wash your hair* |

### Les cosmétiques
*Cosmetics*

| | | | |
|---|---|---|---|
| le maquillage | *make-up* | se sécher les cheveux | *to dry your hair* |
| le démaquillant | *make-up remover* | se maquiller | *to put make-up on* |
| | | se démaquiller | *to remove make-up* |

---

## ENCORE!

● *Activity: Qu'y-a-t-il dans sa trousse de toilette?*
What is in her sponge bag?

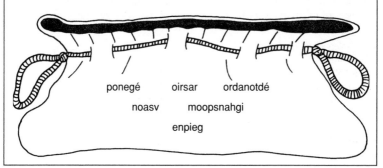

ponegé    oirsar    ordanotdé

noasv    moopsnahgi

enpieg

# 12 Le corps et la santé *The body and health*

## LA MALADIE
### *ILLNESS*

## Bon rétablissement!
### *Get well soon!*

| | |
|---|---|
| la santé | *health* |
| en bonne santé | *fit / healthy* |
| contagieux(-ieuse) | |
| | *infectious* |
| la maladie $\left\{\begin{array}{l}\end{array}\right.$ | *disease* |
| | *illness* |
| | *sickness* |
| la fièvre | *fever* |
| malade $\left\{\begin{array}{l}\end{array}\right.$ | *ill* |
| | *sick* |
| la douleur | *pain* |
| le médicament | *medicine* |
| douloureux | |
| (-euse) | *sore / painful* |

### Les maladies et les problèmes de santé
*Illnesses and indisposition*

| | |
|---|---|
| le SIDA | *Aids* |
| l'anorexie (f.) | *anorexia* |
| l'appendicite (f.) | *appendicitis* |
| l'arthrite (f.) | *arthritis* |
| l'asthme (m.) | *asthma* |
| la mycose | *athlete's foot* |
| l'ampoule (f.) | *blister* |
| le furoncle | *boil* |
| la jambe cassée | *broken leg* |
| le bras cassé | *broken arm* |
| le bleu | *bruising* |
| la boulimie | *bulimia* |
| la brûlure | *burn* |
| le cancer | *cancer* |
| la cataracte | *cataract* |
| le rhume chronique | *catarrh* |
| la cellulite | *cellulite* |

| | |
|---|---|
| la varicelle | *chicken pox* |
| le choléra | *cholera* |
| la constipation | *constipation* |
| la dermatite | *dermatitis* |
| le diabète | *diabetes* |
| la diarrhée | *diarrhoea* |
| la diphtérie | *diphtheria* |
| l'eczéma (m.) | *eczema* |
| la rubéole | *German measles* |
| la grippe | *flu / influenza* |
| l'hémophilie (f.) | *haemophilia* |
| l'hémorragie (f.) | *haemorrhage* |
| les hémorroïdes (f. pl.) | *haemorrhoids* |
| la mauvaise haleine | *halitosis* |
| les brûlures d'estomac (f. pl.) | *heart burn* |
| l'hépatite (f.) | *hepatitis* |
| la hernie | *hernia* |
| l'hypertension (f.) | *high blood pressure* |
| l'hypotension (f.) | *low blood pressure* |
| séropositif porteur sain $\left.\begin{array}{l}\end{array}\right\}$ | *HIV positive* |
| séronégatif | *HIV negative* |
| le traitement hormonal substitutif | *HRT* |
| l'indigestion (f.) | *indigestion* |
| la contagion la contamination $\left.\begin{array}{l}\end{array}\right\}$ | *infection* |
| les démangeaisons (f. pl.) | *itching* |
| la malaria | *malaria* |
| la rougeole | *measles* |
| la méningite | *meningitis* |
| la ménopause | *menopause* |
| les oreillons (m. pl.) | *mumps* |
| la douleur articulaire | *muscular pain* |
| l'obésité (f.) | *obesity* |

| | | | |
|---|---|---|---|
| les douleurs menstruelles (f. pl.) | *period pain* | handicappé(e) | *handicapped* |
| | | boiteux (-euse) | *lame* |
| le syndrome prémenstruel | *PMT* | aveugle | *blind* |
| | | sourd(e) | *deaf* |
| la polio | *polio* | muet/muette | *dumb* |
| la rage | *rabies* | paraplégique | *paraplegic* |
| le rhumatisme | *rheumatism* | le fauteuil roulant | *wheel chair* |
| la croûte | *scab* | le membre artificiel, la prothèse | *artificial limb* |
| la cicatrice | *scar* | | |
| le choc | *shock* | | |
| le stress | *stress* | la maladie chronique | *chronic illness* |
| la crise cardiaque | *stroke* | spasmodique | *spasmodic* |
| le coup de soleil | *sunburn* | | |
| l'insolation (f.) | *sunstroke* | le docteur | *doctor* |
| la tuberculose | *TB* | le / la pédicure | *chiropodist* |
| la température } la fièvre } | *temperature* | l'orthopédiste (m. f.) | *orthopaedic surgeon* |
| le tétanos | *tetanus* | l'ostéopathe (m. f.) | *osteopath* |
| le muguet | *thrush* | le / la physiothérapeute, le / la kinésithérapeute } | *physiotherapist* |
| le mal des transports | *travel sickness* | | |
| la maladie vénérienne | *VD, veneral disease* | le chiropracteur | *chiropractor* |
| | | l'opticien(ne) | *optician* |
| l'infection (f.) | *infection* | l'infirmière (f.) | *nurse* |
| la bactérie | *bacteria* | l'infirmier (m.) | *male nurse* |
| le virus | *virus* | le cabinet médical | *surgery* |
| | | le rendez-vous | *appointment* |

### Chez le médecin
*At the doctor's*

| | |
|---|---|
| Je peux prendre rendez-vous? | *Can I make an appointment?* |
| J'ai mal au cœur | *I feel sick* |
| Je ne me sens pas bien | *ill* |
| J'ai un rhume | *I have a cold* |
| Je tousse | *cough* |
| J'ai mal à la gorge | *sore throat* |
| J'ai de la température | *temperature* |

## 12 Le corps et la santé *The body and health*

J'ai mal à l'estomac | *I have stomach ache*
Je voudrais quelque chose pour ... | *Can I have something for ...*

prendre la tension | *to take one's blood pressure*
prendre un échantillon | *to take a sample*
faire une prise de sang | *to take a blood sample*
prendre la température | *to take one's temperature*
prendre le pouls | *to take one's pulse*
prescrire un traitement | *to prescribe treatment*
prescrire des médicaments | *to prescribe medication*
consulter un spécialiste | *to refer to a consultant*

### Chez le dentiste
*At the dentist*

le cabinet dentaire | *dental surgery*
le dentiste | *dentist*
l'assistante dentaire | *dental nurse*

la gencive | *gum*
la dent | *tooth*
la racine | *root*
l'incisive (f.) | *incisor*

la canine | *canine*
la molaire | *molar*
la dent de sagesse | *wisdom tooth*

la mâchoire supérieure / inférieure | *upper / lower jaw*
la dent de lait | *milk tooth*
les fausses dents (f. pl.) | *false teeth, dentures*
le plombage | *filling*
la couronne | *cap, crown*
l'appareil dentaire (m.) | *brace*
la brosse à dents | *toothbrush*
le dentifrice | *toothpaste*
le fil dentaire | *dental floss*
le cure-dent | *tooth pick*
le bain de bouche, l'élixir dentaire (m.) | *mouth wash*

J'ai mal aux dents | *I have a toothache*
un abcès | *an abscess*
une dent sensible | *a sensitive tooth*
J'ai perdu/cassé une dent | *I have lost / broken a tooth*
un plombage | *filling*
une couronne | *cap*
un bridge | *bridge*

## 12 Le corps et la santé *The body and health*

**TRAITEMENT ET REMÈDES**
*TREATMENT AND*
*REMEDIES*

### Le premier secours *First aid*

| | |
|---|---|
| le pansement | |
| le bandage | |
| le pansement adhésif | } *bandage* |
| le sparadrap | *sticking plaster* |
| la pince à épiler | *tweezers* |
| la compresse | *lint* |
| l'épingle à nourrice (f.) | *safety pin* |
| la blessure | *wound* |
| l'écharpe (f.) | *sling* |
| le plâtre | *plaster / cast* |

### Les remèdes *Medicines*

| | |
|---|---|
| les antibiotiques (m. pl.) | *antibiotics* |
| la crème | *cream* |
| la crème antihistaminique | *antihistamine cream* |
| les comprimés anti-inflammatoires (m. pl.) | *anti-inflammatory tablets* |
| les comprimés contre la malaria | *anti-malaria tablets* |
| la crème antiseptique | *antiseptic cream* |
| le pansement | *dressing* |
| les gouttes (f. pl.) | *drops* |
| l'infusion (f.) | *infusion* |
| l'inhalateur (m.) | *inhaler* |
| les pastilles (f. pl.) | *lozenges* |
| le pessaire | *pessary* |
| le diaphragme | *the diaphragm* |
| la pilule | *the (contraceptive) pill* |

| | |
|---|---|
| les comprimés (m. pl.) | *pills* |
| les somnifères (m. pl.) | *sleeping pills* |
| les gélules (f. pl.) | *capsules* |
| les suppositoires (m. pl.) | *suppositories* |
| les tranquillisants (m. pl.) | *tranquillisers* |

### Autres remèdes
*Other remedies*

| | |
|---|---|
| l'acupuncture (f.) | *acupuncture* |
| le shiatsu | *acupressure* |
| l'homéopathie (f.) | *homeopathy* |
| l'aromathérapie (f.) | *aromatherapy* |
| la réflexologie | *reflexology* |
| la radiologie | *radiology* |
| les médicines naturelles (f. pl.) | *natural remedies* |
| la physiothérapie la kinésithérapie | } *physiotherapy* |
| le régime | *diet* |
| le régime à base de fibres | *dietary fibre* |
| l'alimentation saine (f.) | *healthy eating* |

| | |
|---|---|
| perdre / prendre du poids | *to lose / gain weight* |
| faire de l'exercice | *to exercise* |
| jeûner | *to fast* |
| s'étouffer | *to choke* |
| stériliser | *to sterilise* |
| infecter | *to infect* |
| souffrir | *to suffer* |
| s'évanouir | *to faint* |

## 12 Le corps et la santé *The body and health*

### L'HÔPITAL
*HOSPITAL*

| | |
|---|---|
| la clinique | *clinic* |
| l'ambulance (f.) | *ambulance* |
| le / la chirurgien (-ienne) | *surgeon* |
| le / la spécialiste | *consultant* |
| le / la gynécologue | *gynaecologist* |
| le / la pédiatre | *paediatrician* |
| l'orthodontiste (m. f.) | *orthodontist* |
| le docteur | *doctor* |
| l'infirmier (-ière) | *nurse* |
| le / la malade | *patient* |

| | |
|---|---|
| le lit | *bed* |
| le pavillon le service } | *ward* |
| le brancard | *stretcher* |
| la convalescence | *convalescence* |
| le rétablissement | *recuperation* |
| vacciner { | *to vaccinate* / *to inoculate* |
| faire mal | *to hurt* |
| se sentir mal | *to feel ill* |
| se sentir bien | *to feel well* |
| aller mieux | *to improve* |
| se rétablir | *to convalesce* |
| opérer | *to operate* |
| plâtrer | *to plaster* |
| avoir mal au cœur | *to feel sick* |
| vomir | *to vomit* |

| | |
|---|---|
| l'opération (f.) | *operation* |
| la salle d'opération | *operating theatre* |
| l'anesthésie locale / générale (f.) | *local / general anaesthetic* |
| l'anesthésiste (m. f.) | *anaesthetist* |
| la radio | *X-ray* |
| la perfusion | *drip* |
| l'injection intraveineuse (f.) | *intravenous medicine* |
| l'intervention chirurgicale (f.) | *surgery* |
| le laser | *laser* |
| le scalpel | *scalpel* |
| les instruments (m. pl.) | *instruments* |

## 12 Le corps et la santé *The body and health*

### L'ALCOOL, LE TABAC ET LES DROGUES
*ALCOHOL, SMOKING AND DRUGS*

Défense de fumer

| | |
|---|---|
| alcoolique | *alcholic* |
| l'empoisonnement par l'alcool (m.) | *alcohol poisoning* |
| Les Alcooliques Anonymes | *Alcoholics Anonymous* |
| Les Samaritains | *The Samaritans* |
| Il/elle boit trop | *He / she drinks too much* |
| a trop bu | *is over the limit* |

| | |
|---|---|
| l'emphysème (m.) | *emphysema* |
| le cancer | *cancer* |
| s'arrêter de fumer | *to give up smoking* |
| réduire | *to cut down* |
| le / la toxicomane<br>le / la drogué(e) } | *drug addict* |

| | |
|---|---|
| le / la fumeur (-euse) | *smoker* |
| le / la non-fumeur (-euse) | *non-smoker* |
| les cigarettes (f. pl.) | *cigarettes* |
| les cigares (m. pl.) | *cigars* |
| la pipe | *pipe* |
| le tabac | *tobacco* |
| le briquet | *lighter* |
| les allumettes (f. pl.) | *matches* |
| le papier à cigarettes | *cigarette paper* |
| le cendrier | *ashtray* |
| la nicotine | *nicotine* |

| | |
|---|---|
| les drogues (f. pl.) | *drugs* |
| le cannabis | *cannabis* |
| le hashish | *hashish* |
| la cocaïne | *cocaine* |
| le crack | *crack* |
| l'héroïne (f.) | *heroin* |
| la seringue | *syringe* |
| la toxicomanie | *drug addiction* |
| le manque | *withdrawal symptoms*<br>*cold turkey* |
| fumer | *to smoke* |
| avaler (la fumée) | *to inhale* |
| injecter | *to inject* |

| | |
|---|---|
| se faire désintoxiquer | *to dry out* |
| être en état de manque | *to experience withdrawal symptoms* |

# 13 Les institutions *Institutions*

## LA BANQUE ET LA FINANCE *BANKING AND FINANCE*
### L'argent et la banque *Money and the bank*

| | |
|---|---|
| la caisse d'épargne | *savings bank* |
| la société de prêt immobilier | *building society* |
| le compte bancaire | *bank account* |
| le distributeur automatique | *cash machine* |
| la carte d'identité bancaire | *cheque card* |
| le taux de change | *exchange rate* |
| la pièce d'identité | *identification* |
| les livres sterling (f.pl.) | *pounds sterling* |

| | | | | |
|---|---|---|---|---|
| la banque | *bank* | créditeur | *in credit* |
| l'agence (f.) | *branch* | à découvert | *in the red, overdrawn* |
| le solde | *balance* | l'emprunt (m.) | *loan* |
| les agios (m.pl.) | *bank charges* | l'argent (m.) | *money* |
| le code guichet | *bank sort code* | le prêt | |
| l'employé(e) | | immobilier | *mortgage* |
| de banque | *cashier* | les billets (m.pl.) | *notes* |
| la monnaie | *change* | le découvert | *overdraft* |
| le chèque | *cheque* | le compte | |
| le crédit | *credit* | épargne | *savings account* |
| la carte de | | le livret | |
| crédit | *credit card* | épargne | *savings book* |
| la monnaie | *currency* | la signature | *signature* |
| le compte | | le relevé de | |
| courant | *current account* | compte | *statement* |
| le débit | *debit* | la caisse | *till* |
| le dépôt | *deposit* | le transfert | *transfer* |
| le compte sur | | le retrait | *withdrawal* |
| livret | *deposit account* | | |

| | |
|---|---|
| le chèque de voyage } le traveller | *traveller's cheque* |
| le chèque barré | *crossed cheque* |
| le chèque en blanc | *blank cheque* |
| le chèque non validé | *invalid cheque* |
| le chèque non barré | *open cheque* |
| le mandat postal | *postal order* |
| la falsification | *forgery* |

# 13 Les institutions *Institutions*

| | |
|---|---|
| emprunter | *to borrow* |
| encaisser un chèque | *to cash a cheque* |
| changer de l'argent | *to change money* |
| faire un dépôt | *to deposit* |
| prêter | *to lend* |
| rembourser | *to pay back, repay* |
| déposer | *to pay in* |
| falsifier | *to forge* |

## La finance *Finance*

| | |
|---|---|
| le capital | { *assets* |
| | { *capital* |
| le budget | *budget* |
| l'acte (m.) | *certificate* |
| le coût de la vie | *cost of living* |
| la dette | *debt* |
| la dépréciation | *depreciation* |
| les dépenses (f.pl.) | *expenses* |
| l'indice (m.) | *index* |
| l'inflation (f.) | *inflation* |
| les intérêts (m.pl.) | *interest* |
| l'investissement (m.) | *investment* |
| le prêt | *loan* |
| le paiement | *payment* |
| le pourcentage | *percentage* |
| le profit | *profit* |
| l'achat (m.) | *purchase* |
| le reçu | *receipt* |
| la vente | *sale* |
| l'action (f.) | *share* |
| les valeurs (f.pl.) | *stocks* |
| la somme | *sum* |
| la valeur | *value* |

| | |
|---|---|
| la Bourse | *Stock Exchange* |
| le marché à la baisse | *bear market* |
| le marché à la hausse | *bull market* |
| les actions (f.pl.) | *stocks and shares* |
| l'industrie minière (f.) | *mining* |
| l'industrie pharmaceutique | *pharmaceuticals* |
| la commerce | *trade* |
| les fonds (m.pl) | *funds* |
| les réserves (f.pl.) | *stores* |
| l'industrie de fabrication | *manufacturing* |
| les matières premières | *commodities* |
| les assurances (f.pl.) | *insurance* |
| la banque | *banking* |
| l'impôt (m.) | *tax* |
| l'impôt sur le revenu | *income tax* |
| la TVA | *VAT* |
| les sommes déductibles (f.pl.) | *allowances* |

# 13 Les institutions *Institutions*

## Les monnaies *Currencies*

| | |
|---|---|
| la monnaie | *currency* |
| le billet | *note* |
| la pièce | *coin* |
| l'argent liquide (m.) | *cash* |
| le dollar américain | *American dollar* |

| | |
|---|---|
| le dollar australien | *Australian dollar* |
| la livre sterling | *pound sterling* |
| le franc | *franc* |
| le franc suisse | *Swiss franc* |
| le deutschmark | *Deutschmark* |
| la lire | *lira* |
| la peseta | *peseta* |
| le yen | *yen* |

| | |
|---|---|
| valoir | *to be worth* |
| emprunter | *to borrow* |
| acheter | *to buy* |
| prélever des intérêts | *to charge interest* |
| coûter | *to cost* |
| gagner | *to gain* |
| investir | *to invest* |
| prêter | *to lend* |
| perdre | *to lose* |

| | |
|---|---|
| payer | *to pay* |
| payer des taxes | *to pay tax* |
| économiser | *to save* |
| vendre | *to sell* |
| dépenser | *to spend* |
| cher/chère | { *dear* *expensive* |
| bon marché | *cheap* |
| riche/pauvre | *rich / poor* |

# 13 Les institutions *Institutions*

## L'ÉGLISE ET LA RELIGION
### *CHURCH AND RELIGION*

| | |
|---|---|
| la religion | *religion* |
| le christianisme | *Christianity* |
| le bouddhisme | *Buddhism* |
| l'hindouisme (m.) | *Hinduism* |
| l'Islam (m.) | *Islam* |
| le judaïsme | *Judaism* |
| le catholicisme | *Catholicism* |
| le protestantisme | |
| | *Protestantism* |

| | |
|---|---|
| Allah | *Allah* |
| Bouddha | *Buddha* |
| le Christ | *Christ* |
| Dieu | *God* |
| le Saint Esprit | *Holy Ghost* |
| Mohammed | *Mohammed* |
| Moïse | *Moses* |
| l'apôtre (m.) | *apostle* |
| l'archevêque (m.) | *archbishop* |
| l'évêque (m.) | *bishop* |
| le cardinal | *cardinal* |

| | |
|---|---|
| Je suis athée | *I am a / an atheist* |
| agnostique | *agnostic* |
| chrétien (-ienne) | *Christian* |
| bouddhiste | *Buddhist* |
| hindou(e) | *Hindu* |
| musulman(e) | *Moslem* |
| juif/juive | *Jew* |
| catholique | *Roman Catholic* |
| protestant(e) | *Protestant* |
| quaker | *Quaker* |
| Témoin de Jéhovah | *Jehovah's witness* |

| | |
|---|---|
| le disciple | *disciple* |
| l'imam (m.) | *imam* |
| le martyr | *martyr* |
| le Messie | *Messiah* |
| le pasteur | *minister* |
| le moine | *monk* |
| la nonne | *nun* |
| le pèlerin | *pilgrim* |
| le Pape | *pope* |
| le prêtre | *priest* |
| le prophète | *prophet* |
| le rabin | *rabbi* |
| le / la saint(e) | *saint* |
| le pécheur }<br>la pécheresse } | *sinner* |
| l'abbé | *priest / abbot* |
| le curé | *parish priest* |

| | |
|---|---|
| l'office (m.) | *service* |
| la messe | *mass* |
| la communion | *communion* |
| l'hymne (m.) { | *hymn*<br>*anthem* |
| la prière | *prayer* |
| le sermon | *sermon* |
| le psaume | *psalm* |
| la bénédiction | *blessing* |
| l'autel (m.) | *altar* |
| la cathédrale | *cathedral* |
| la chapelle | *chapel* |
| le chœur | *choir* |
| l'église (f.) | *church* |
| la coupole | *cupola* |
| la mosquée | *mosque* |
| la nef | *nave* |

# 13 Les institutions *Institutions*

| | | | |
|---|---|---|---|
| la flèche | *spire* | le miracle | *miracle* |
| le temple | *temple* | le pèlerinage | *pilgrimage* |
| la synagogue | *synagogue* | la guerre sainte | *holy war* |
| | | le jihad | *jihad* |
| la croix | *cross* | | |
| la bougie | *candle* | croire | *to believe* |
| | | ne pas croire | *to not believe* |
| l'ange (m.) | *angel* | aller à l'église | *to attend church* |
| le diable ⎫ | *devil* | chanter | *to sing* |
| le démon ⎭ | | réciter | *to chant* |
| le paradis | *heaven, paradise* | prier | *to pray* |
| l'enfer (m.) | *hell* | vénérer | *to worship* |
| le purgatoire | *purgatory* | se convertir | *to convert* |
| le salut | *salvation* | se confesser | *to confess* |
| la damnation | *damnation* | absoudre | *to absolve* |
| | | prêcher | *to preach* |
| la foi | *faith* | repentir | *to repent* |
| la croyance | *belief* | faire un | *to make a* |
| la création | *creation* | pèlerinage | *pilgrimage* |

# 13 Les institutions *Institutions*

## L'ÉDUCATION
### *EDUCATION*

| | |
|---|---|
| le jardin d'enfant ⎫ la garderie ⎭ | *kindergarten / play school* |
| l'école (f.) | *school* |
| l'école primaire | *primary school* |
| l'école secondaire | *secondary school* |
| le collège | *comprehensive school* |
| le lycée | *sixth form college* |
| le lycée technique | *technical college* |
| l'institut universitaire de technologie (IUT) | *polytechnic* |
| l'université (f.) | *university* |
| l'école primaire privée | *prep school* |
| l'école privée | *private school* |
| l'école publique | *state school* |
| le directeur ⎫ la directrice ⎭ | *headteacher* |
| le sous-directeur ⎫ la sous-directrice ⎭ | *deputy head* |
| le professeur (m.f.) | *teacher* |
| l'instituteur (-trice) | *primary school teacher* |
| l'élève | *pupil (m.f.)* |
| l'étudiant(e) | *student* |
| l'élève chargé de la discipline | *prefect* |
| la secrétaire | *school secretary* |
| le concierge | *caretaker* |
| le / la bibliothécaire | *librarian* |
| l'infirmière (f.) | *nurse* |
| la classe { | *class* / *grade* |
| la leçon ⎫ le cours ⎭ | *lesson* |
| la récréation | *break* |
| l'appel (m.) | *taking the register* |

## Les matières *Subjects*

| | |
|---|---|
| les mathématiques (f.pl.) | *maths* |
| l'anglais (m.) | *English* |
| le français | *French* |
| l'allemand (m.) | *German* |
| l'espagnol (m.) | *Spanish* |
| les sciences (f.pl) | *science* |
| la physique | *physics* |
| la chimie | *chemistry* |
| la biologie | *biology* |
| la géographie | *geography* |
| l'histoire (f.) | *history* |
| l'environnement (m.) | *environmental studies* |
| l'art (m.) | *art* |
| la musique | *music* |
| l'éducation religieuse (f.) | *R.E.* |
| la sociologie | *sociology* |
| le théâtre | *drama* |
| l'éducation physique | *P.E.* |
| la technologie | *technology* |
| l'informatique (f.) | *information technology* |
| l'examen (m.) | *examination* |
| l'examen oral | *oral examination* |
| l'examen écrit | *written examination* |
| les devoirs (m.pl.) | *homework* |
| le devoir écrit | *essay* |
| l'exercice (m.) | *exercise* |
| le dossier | *project* |
| la lecture | *reading* |
| l'écriture | *writing* |
| l'orthographe (f.) | *spelling* |

# 13 Les institutions *Institutions*

la ponctuation    *\*punctuation*
le rapport    *report*
la note    *mark / grade*
*la conduite*    *behaviour*
(\*See also *Arts and the media*,
page 97.)

| | |
|---|---|
| apprendre | *to learn* |
| réviser | *to revise* |
| étudier | *to study* |
| passer un examen | *to sit an exam* |
| réussir un examen | *to pass an exam* |
| échouer à un examen | *to fail an exam* |
| repasser un examen | *to re-sit an exam* |
| | |
| le certificat | *certificate* |
| la qualification | *qualification* |
| la licence | *degree* |
| la maîtrise | *master's degree* |
| le / la diplômé(e) | *graduate* |
|    licencié(e) ès lettres | *Bachelor of Arts* |
|        ès sciences | *of science* |
|        en droit | *of law* |
| le / la titulaire d'une maîtrise | |
|    ès lettres | *Master of Arts* |
| le docteur | *doctor* |
| le professeur | *professor* |

| | | | |
|---|---|---|---|
| les matières à l'université | | les langues vivantes | |
|   (f.pl.) | *university subjects* |   (f.pl.) | *modern languages* |
| le droit | *law* | les langues mortes | |
| la médecine | *medicine* |   (f.pl.) | *classical languages* |
| l'ingénierie (f.) | *engineering* | l'archéologie (f.) | *archaeology* |
| les sciences humaines | | le génie | *mechanical* |
|   (f.pl.) | *humanities* |   mécanique | *engineering* |
| les sciences | | la génie | |
|   (f.pl.) | *sciences* |   électrique | *electrical engineering* |
| la psychologie | *psychology* | l'électronique (f.) | *electronics* |
| la psychiatrie | *psychiatry* | l'informatique | *information* |
| la philosophie | *philosophy* |   (f.) | *technology* |

# 13 Les institutions *Institutions*

l'étudiant(e)   *student*
l'étudiant(e) de première
   année   *fresher*
le cours
   magistral   *lecture*
le maître de
   conférence   *lecturer*
l'amphithéâtre
   (m.)   *lecture theatre*
le/la candidat(e)   *candidate*
l'examinateur
   (m.)   *examiner*
la moyenne   *pass mark*
la copie
   d'examen   *exam paper*

la question   *question*
la réponse   *answer*
le résultat   *result*

les vacances
   (f.pl.)   *holidays*
l'année scolaire
   (f.)   *school year*
la nouvelle
   année scolaire   *new school year*
le jour de congé   *day off*
le trimestre   *term*
la rentrée   *beginning of*
       *school year*

# 13 Les institutions *Institutions*

## LA LOI ET L'ORDRE
### *LAW AND ORDER*

### Les délits et la police
*Crime and the police*

| | |
|---|---|
| le / la complice | *accomplice* |
| l'arrestation (f.) | *arrest* |
| l'incendie criminel (m.) | *arson* |
| le/la pyromane | *arsonist* |
| l'agression (f.) | *assault* |
| l'attaque (f.) | *attack* |
| la tentative | *attempt* |
| le chantage | *blackmail* |
| le cambriolage | *break-in* |
| le voleur | *burglar* |
| l'alarme (f.) | *burglar alarm* |
| le crime | *crime* |
| le/la criminel(le) | *criminal* |
| l'escroc (m.) | *crook* |
| le dealer | *drug dealer* |
| l'urgence (f.) | *emergency* |
| le numéro d'urgence | *emergency number* |
| la bagarre | *fight* |
| l'amende (f.) | *fine* |
| l'usage de faux (m.) | *forgery* |
| la fraude | *fraud* |
| le gang | *gang* |
| les coups et blessures | *grievous bodily harm* |
| le guérilla | *guerrilla* |
| le revolver | *gun, revolver* |
| le casque | *helmet* |
| la prise d'otages | *hi-jacking, hostage-taking* |
| le hold-up | *hold-up* |
| le hooligan le délinquant } | *hooligan / yob* |
| l'otage (m.) | *hostage* |
| l'attentat à la pudeur (m.) | *indecent assault* |
| le kidnapping | *kidnapping* |
| le meurtrier | *murderer* |
| le narcotique | *narcotics* |
| le pickpocket | *pickpocket* |
| le pistolet | *pistol* |
| le braconnier | *poacher* |
| le poison | *poison* |
| la voiture de police | *police car* |
| le policier | *policeman / officer* |
| la femme policier | *policewoman* |
| la rançon | *ransom* |
| le receveur | *receiver* |
| le vol | *robbery* |
| le système de sécurité | *security system* |
| les violences sexuelles (f.pl) | *sexual attack* |
| le vol à l'étalage | *shoplifting* |
| l'espion (f.) | *spy* |
| le / la terroriste | *terrorist* |
| le voleur | *thief* |
| le traitre | *traitor* |
| l'uniforme (m.) | *uniform* |
| l'arme (f.) | *weapon* |
| attaquer | *to attack* |
| cambrioler | *to burgle* |
| tricher | *to cheat* |
| tromper | *to deceive* |
| braquer | *to hold up* |
| tuer | *to kill* |
| agresser | *to mug* |
| assassiner | *to murder* |
| poursuivre en justice | *to prosecute* |
| violer | *to rape* |
| perquisitionner | *to search* |
| tirer | *to shoot* |
| espionner | *to spy* |
| poignarder | *to stab* |
| voler | *to steal* |
| menacer | *to threaten* |

# 13 Les institutions *Institutions*

## Au tribunal *In court*

| | |
|---|---|
| l'acquittement (m.) | *acquittal* |
| l'appel (m.) | *appeal* |
| la liberté sous caution | *bail* |
| l'affaire (f.) | *brief* |
| le cas | *case* |
| la cellule | *cell* |
| les charges (f.pl.) | *charge* |
| le greffier | *clerk of the court* |
| la plainte | *complaint* |
| les frais judiciaires (f.pl.) | *costs* |
| les dommages et intérêts (m.pl.) | *damages* |
| le jugement provisoire de divorce | *decree nisi* |
| l'amende (f.) | *fine* |
| la culpabilité | *guilt* |
| le / la coupable | *guilty person* |
| l'innocent(e) | *innocent person* |
| l'interrogatoire (m.) | *interrogation* |
| le juge | *judge* |
| le jury | *jury* |
| la loi | *law* |

| | |
|---|---|
| le palais de justice | *law court* |
| le jugement de la cour de justice | *law court trial* |
| l'avocat(e) | *lawyer* |
| le délit mineur | *minor offence* |
| le serment | *oath* |
| le délit l'infraction (f.) | *offence* |
| la prison | *prison* |
| le/la prisonnier (-ière) | *prisoner* |
| l'accusation (f.) | *prosecution* |
| le procès-verbal | *report* |
| la peine | *sentence* |
| le notaire | *solicitor* |
| le verdict | *verdict* |
| le mandat | *warrant* |
| le témoin | *witness* |
| confesser | *confess* |
| la barre des témoins | *box witness* |
| prêter serment | *to swear* |
| plaider coupable | *to plead guilty* |
| plaider non coupable | *to plead innocent* |
| témoigner | *to stand witness* |
| être témoin de | *to witness* |

# 13 Les institutions *Institutions*

| | |
|---|---|
| les forces armées (f.pl.) | *the armed forces* |
| les forces spéciales | *special forces* |
| les forces des Nations Unies | *United Nations forces* |
| la guerre | *war* |
| déclarer la guerre | *to declare war* |
| la paix | *peace* |
| signer un traité de paix | *to sign a peace treaty* |

| | |
|---|---|
| le blocus | *blockade* |
| le coup d'état | *coup* |
| le cessez-le-feu | *ceasefire* |
| l'assaut (m.) | *assault* |
| l'attaque (f.) | *attack* |
| la retraite | *retreat* |
| le retrait | *withdrawal* |
| le guérillero | *guerrilla* (soldier) |
| la guérilla | *guerrilla war* |
| le / la terroriste | *terrorist* |
| la surveillance | *surveillance* |
| les sanctions (f.pl.) | *sanctions* |
| l'accord (m.) | *agreement* |
| la menace | *threat* |
| le casque | *helmet* |
| le véhicule | *vehicle* |
| le transport de troupes | *personnel carrier* |
| se rendre | *surrender* |
| militaire | *military (adj)* |

## L'armée *Army*

| | |
|---|---|
| l'artillerie (f.) | *artillery* |
| la caserne | *barracks* |
| le colonel | *colonel* |
| le camp | *camp* |
| la commande | *command* |
| la compagnie | *company* |
| la cour martial | *court martial* |

| | |
|---|---|
| le maréchal | *field marshal* |
| le général | *general* |
| le Q.G. (Quartier Général) | *HQ* |
| l'officier (m.) | *officer* |
| les autres grades (m.pl.) | *other ranks* |
| la patrouille | *patrol* |
| le grade | *rank* |
| le recru | *recruit* |
| la sentinelle | *sentry* |
| le soldat | *soldier* |
| le tank | *tank* |
| les troupes (f.pl.) | *troops* |

## La marine *Navy*

| | |
|---|---|
| l'amiral (m.) | *admiral* |
| le porte-avions | *aircraft carrier* |
| le cuirassé | *battleship* |
| le capitaine | *captain* |
| le chef mécanicien | *chief engineer* |
| l'équipage (m.) | *crew* |
| le croiseur | *cruiser* |
| la flotte | *fleet* |
| la frégate | *frigate* |
| l'arsenal (m.) | *naval dockyard* |
| le pilote | *pilot* |

# 13 Les institutions *Institutions*

| | |
|---|---|
| le marin | *sailor* |
| le quart | *watch* |

### Les forces aériennes
*Air force*

| | |
|---|---|
| la base aéronavale | *air force base* |
| l'aviateur (m.) | *airman* |
| le co-pilote | *co-pilot* |
| le chasseur | *fighter (plane)* |
| l'hélicoptère (m.) | *helicopter* |
| le jet | *jet* |
| l'entretien (m.) | *maintenance* |
| le navigateur | *navigator* |
| le pilote | *pilot* |
| le radar | *radar* |
| l'escadron (m.) | *squadron* |
| | |
| voler | *to fly* |
| | |
| bombarder | *to bomb* |
| défendre | *to defend* |

### Les armes *Weapons*

| | |
|---|---|
| la bombe | *bomb* |
| le missile guidé | *guided missile* |
| le fusil / revolver / pistolet | *gun* |
| la grenade | *hand grenade* |
| la mitraillette | *machine gun* |
| la mine | *mine* |
| le missile | *missile* |
| le mortier | *mortar* |
| le revolver | *revolver* |
| le fusil | *rifle* |
| l'obus (m.) | *shell* |
| la cible | *target* |
| la torpille | *torpedo* |
| | |
| se battre | *to fight* |
| tirer | *to shoot* |

# 13 Les institutions *Institutions*

## LA POLITIQUE ET LE GOUVERNEMENT
### *POLITICS AND GOVERNMENT*

### L'administration locale   *Local government*

| | |
|---|---|
| la mairie | *town hall* |
| le conseil municipal | *town council* |
| la réunion du conseil municipal | *council meeting* |
| le conseiller municipal | *town councillor* |
| les élus municipaux (m.pl.) | *elected representatives* |
| le maire | *mayor (m. f.)* |
| l'adjoint(e) au maire | *chief executive* |
| le trésorier | *financial officer* |
| les contributions (f.pl.) | *rates* |
| les impôts locaux (m.pl.) | *local taxes* |
| A.N.P.E. (Agence Nationale Pour l'Emploi) | *employment office* |
| les services sociaux (m.pl.) | *social services* |

### Le gouvernement   *National government*

| | |
|---|---|
| la circonscription | *constituency* |
| l'élection (f.) | *election* |
| l'économie (f.) | *economy* |
| le gouvernement | *government* |
| le député | *member of parliament* |
| le ministre de la défense | *minister of defence* |
| du travail | *employment* |
| des transports | *transport* |
| de la santé | *health and safety* |
| de l'éducation | *education* |
| de l'agriculture | *agriculture* |
| le ministre des finances | *minister of finance (Chancellor of the Exchequer)* |
| le ministère | *Ministry* |
| le parlement | *parliament* |
| le parti | *party* |
| l'homme politique } la femme politique } | *politician* |
| le président | *president* |
| le premier ministre | *prime minister* |
| le mandat parlementaire | *seat of parliament* |

# 13 Les institutions *Institutions*

l'ambassadeur
  (-drice)     *ambassador*
le consul     *consul*
le diplomate     *diplomat*
le / la représentant(e)
        *envoy*
l'ambassade (f.) *embassy*

mener une
  campagne     *to canvass*
voter     *to vote*
faire un
  discours     *to speak*
débattre     *to debate*

# 14 La ville et les achats *Town and shopping*

| | |
|---|---|
| la ville | *town; city* |
| la ville industrielle | *industrial town* |
| le port | *port* |
| la ville historique | *historical town* |
| la ville universitaire | *university town* |

## LE CENTRE-VILLE
### *THE TOWN CENTRE*

| | |
|---|---|
| le musée d'art | *art gallery* |
| l'avenue (f.) | *avenue* |
| la banque | *bank* |
| le bar | *bar* |
| le jardin botanique | *botanical gardens* |
| la société de prêt immobilier | *building society* |
| la gare routière | *bus station* |
| le café | *café* |
| le parking | *car park* |
| le cinéma | *cinema* |
| la salle de concerts | *concert hall* |
| la mairie annexe | *council office* |
| le stade de foot | *football stadium* |
| le coiffeur | *hairdresser's* |
| le centre de loisirs | *leisure centre* |
| la bibliothèque | *library* |
| le marché | *market* |

| | |
|---|---|
| la place du marché | *market place* |
| le musée | *museum* |
| le parc | *park* |
| la poste | *post office* |
| le restaurant | *restaurant* |
| la cafétéria ⎫ | *self service* |
| le self ⎭ | *restaurant* |
| la gare | *station* |
| la piscine | *swimming pool* |
| le théâtre | *theatre* |
| l'office de tourisme (m.) | *tourist office* |
| la mairie | *town hall* |
| le zoo | *zoo* |

| | |
|---|---|
| la piste cyclable | *bicycle track* |
| l'arrêt de bus (m.) | *bus stop* |
| l'intersection (f.) | *intersection* |
| le milieu de la route | *middle of the road* |
| le trottoir | *pavement* |
| la zone piétonne | *pedestrian area* |
| le passage clouté | *pedestrian crossing* |
| le passage à niveau | *level crossing* |
| la route | *road* |
| le rond-point | *roundabout* |
| le panneau | *sign post* |
| la rue | *street* |
| le souterrain | *subway* |
| les feux (m.pl.) | *traffic lights* |

# 14  La ville et les achats *Town and shopping*

## LES MAGASINS ET LES ACHATS
### *SHOPS AND SHOPPING*

| | |
|---|---|
| la boulangerie | *bakery* |
| l'esthéticienne (f.) | *beautician* |
| la boucherie | *butcher's* |
| la pâtisserie | *cake shop* |
| le magasin de vêtements | *clothes shop* |
| le grand magasin | *department store* |
| la poissonnerie | *fish shop* |
| le fleuriste | *flower shop* |
| le magasin de fruits et légumes | *greengrocer's* |
| l'épicerie (f.) | *grocer's* |
| le coiffeur | *hairdresser's* |
| la quincaillerie | *ironmonger's* |
| le marchand de journaux | *newsagent's* |
| l'animalerie (f.) | *pet shop* |
| le photographe | *photographer's* |
| le magasin de chaussures | *shoe shop* |
| la papeterie | *stationer's* |
| la confiserie | *sweet shop* |
| le tabac | *tobacconist* |

| | |
|---|---|
| à côté de | *next door to* |
| en face (du cinéma) | *opposite (the cinema)* |
| dans la première à gauche | *in the first (street) on the left* |
| la prochaine à droite | *next street on the right* |
| après les feux | *after the lights* |
| de l'autre côté de la rue | { *across the road* / *on the other side of the road* |
| sur la place du marché | *in the marketplace* |
| sur la place | *on the square* |
| sur la route de ... } dans la rue de ... } | *in the ... road / street* |
| là-bas | *over there* |
| au coin de | *on the corner of* |

## Faire les courses *Shopping*

| | |
|---|---|
| Je voudrais ... | *I would like ...* |
| Avez-vous une bouteille de ...? | *Have you got a bottle of ...?* |
| un pot de | *jar of* |
| une boîte de | *box of* |
| un paquet de | *packet of* |
| un tube de | *tube of* |
| une caisse de | *case of* |
| un bidon de | *drum of* |
| une boîte de | *can / tin of* |
| un sachet de | *sachet of* |

# 14 **La ville et les achats** *Town and shopping*

| | |
|---|---|
| frais/fraîche | *fresh* |
| en boîte | *tinned* |
| avarié(e) | *stale* |
| cru(e) / cuit(e) | *raw / cooked* |
| C'est combien? | |
| Ça coûte combien? | *How much does it cost?* |
| C'est tout. | *That's all.* |
| Merci. | *Thank you.* |
| Je suis desolé(e) mais je n'ai pas | |
|    de monnaie. Pardon. | *I'm sorry, I haven't any change.* |
| la demi-livre | *250 grammes (approx. ½ lb)* |
| la livre | *a pound (1lb)* |
| le demi-kilo | *500 grammes (approx. 1lb)* |
| le kilo | *kilogramme* |
| le centilitre | *10 millilitres* |
| le décilitre | *100 millilitres* |
| le demi-litre | *half a litre (approx. 1 pint)* |
| le litre | *litre* |

# 14 La ville et les achats *Town and shopping*

## AU GRAND MAGASIN
### *IN THE DEPARTMENT STORE*

### Sous-sol *Basement*

| | |
|---|---|
| le traiteur ⎫ | *Delicatessen* |
| l'épicerie fine (f.) ⎭ | |
| les arts de la table (m.pl.) | *Kitchenware* |
| le bricolage | *DIY* |

### Rez-de-chaussée *Ground floor*

| | |
|---|---|
| la maroquinerie | *Leather goods* |
| la papeterie | *Stationery* |
| la hi-fi | *Music and Radio* |
| l'agence de voyages (f.) | *Travel agent* |
| le snack bar | *Snack bar* |
| la parfumerie | *Perfumery* |
| les cosmétiques (m.pl.) | *Cosmetics* |
| les vêtements hommes | *Menswear* |
| la photographie | *Photography* |

### Premier étage *First floor*

| | |
|---|---|
| les vêtements femmes | *Women's wear* |
| la lingerie | *Underwear* |
| les robes (f.pl.) | *Dresses* |
| les costumes (m.pl.) | *Suits* |
| les coordonnés (m.pl.) | *Separates* |
| les vêtements sport (m.pl.) | *Casual wear* |
| la tenue de soirée | *Evening wear* |

### Deuxième étage *Second floor*

| | |
|---|---|
| la décoration d'intérieur | *Home furnishings* |
| le linge de maison ⎰ | *Bed linen* |
| ⎱ | *Household linen* |
| la vaisselle | *China and glassware* |
| la coutellerie | *Cutlery* |
| les sports et vêtements de sports (m.pl.) | *Sports and sportswear* |
| les vêtements enfants et jouets (m.pl.) | *Childrenswear and toys* |

# 14 La ville et les achats *Town and shopping*

## Troisième étage *Third floor*

| | |
|---|---|
| les meubles (m.pl.) | *Furniture* |
| les revêtements de sol (m.pl.) | *Carpeting and flooring* |
| les appareils électriques (m.pl.) | *Electrical goods* |
| les ordinateurs (m.pl.) | *Computers* |
| les télévisions (f.pl.) et les vidéos (m.pl.) | *Television and video* |

## Quatrième étage *Fourth floor*

| | |
|---|---|
| le restaurant | *Restaurant* |
| le service après-vente | *Customer services* |
| les toilettes (f.pl.) | *Toilets* |
| les bureaux (m.pl.) | *Offices* |

## Où aller dans un magasin *Directions in a store*

| | |
|---|---|
| Où est l'ascenseur (m.)? | *Where is the lift?* |
| le rayon | *shelf* |
| l'allée (f.) | *row* |
| le rayon | *department* |
| l'étage (m.) | *floor* |
| la caisse | *counter, till* |
| le sous-sol | *basement* |
| l'escalator (m.) | *escalator* |
| la sortie | *exit* |

## Faire des achats *Making purchases*

| | |
|---|---|
| C'est combien? | *How much is it?* |
| C'est trop. | *It's too much.* |
| cher / chère | *expensive* |
| bon marché | *cheap* |
| trop grand(e) / petit(e) | *too big / small* |
| abimé(e) | *damaged* |
| Vous avez quelque chose ...? | *Have you got anything ...?* |
| de moins cher | *cheaper* |
| de plus cher | *more expensive* |
| de plus grand | *bigger* |

# 14 La ville et les achats *Town and shopping*

| | |
|---|---|
| de mieux | *better* |
| en rouge | *in red* |
| | |
| Ça vient d'où? | *Where is it / are they from?* |
| C'est fait en quoi? | *What is it / are they made of?* |
| Je peux essayer? | *Can I try it on?* |
| Où sont les cabines d'essayage? | *Where are the changing rooms?* |
| Avez-vous une taille plus grande? | *Have you got a size bigger?* |
| petite | *smaller* |
| quelquechose de plus large | *something wider* |
| plus étroit | *narrower* |
| plus long | *longer* |
| plus court | *shorter* |
| | |
| J'aime. | *I like it.* |
| Je n'aime pas. | *I don't like it.* |
| Ça va. | *It fits.* |
| Ça ne va pas. | *It doesn't fit.* |
| Ça me va. | *It suits me.* |
| Ça ne me va pas. | *It doesn't suit me.* |
| La couleur me va. | *The colour suits me.* |
| Le style ne me va pas. | *The style doesn't suit me.* |
| Je le/la prends. | *I'll take it.* |
| Je peux en commander un(e)? | *Can I order one?* |
| Je paye où? | *Where do I pay?* |
| Prenez-vous les cartes de crédit? | *Do you take credit cards?* |
| Prenez-vous les chèques? | *Do you take cheques?* |
| Je n'ai pas de monnaie. | *I haven't any change.* |

# 14 La ville et les achats *Town and shopping*

## CHEZ LE COIFFEUR
### *AT THE HAIRDRESSER'S*

| | |
|---|---|
| les cheveux (m.pl.) | |
| | *hair* |
| la permanente | *perm* |
| l'ondulation (f.) | *wave* |
| la frange | *fringe* |

| | |
|---|---|
| la perruque | *wig* |
| le toupet | *hair piece* |
| la natte | *plait* |
| la queue | |
| de cheval | *pony tail* |
| la coupe | |
| au carré | *pageboy* |

| | |
|---|---|
| les cheveux courts/longs | *short / long hair* |
| ondulés/frisés | *wavy / curly* |
| raides | *straight* |
| brillants | *shiny* |
| le shampooing | *shampoo* |
| le baume démêlant | *conditioner* |
| les ciseaux (m.pl.) | *scissors* |
| le rasoir | *razor* |
| | |
| couper | *to cut* |
| laver | *to wash* |
| sécher | *to blow dry* |
| friser | *to curl* |
| se teindre les cheveux | *to dye your hair* |
| se faire faire une couleur | *to have your hair coloured* |
| se faire faire une permanente | *to have your hair permed* |
| se décolorer les cheveux | *to bleach your hair* |

## *ENCORE!*

● *Activity: How do you want your hair?*

Je les veux . . .

# 14 La ville et les achats *Town and shopping*

## À LA BANQUE ET À LA POSTE
### *AT THE BANK AND POST OFFICE*

Les timbres à validité permanente sont valables, quelle que soit l'évolution des tarifs, pour une lettre de 20 grammes pour la FRANCE, les DOM-TOM, la CEE, l'AUTRICHE, le LIECHTENSTEIN et la SUISSE

*LA POSTE*

**10 TIMBRES-POSTE**
**À**
VALIDITÉ PERMANENTE
**AUTOCOLLANTS**

| | |
|---|---|
| la banque | *bank* |
| les heures d'ouverture (f.pl.) | *opening hours* |
| le / la caissier (-ière) | *cashier / teller* |
| le guichet | { *counter* / *position* |
| la caisse | *cash desk* |
| le change | { *money exchange* / *foreign transactions* |
| le chèque | *cheque* |

| | |
|---|---|
| la carte de crédit | *credit card (f.pl.)* |
| les espèces / l'argent liquide (m.) | } *cash* |
| les billets (m.pl.) | *notes* |
| les pièces (f.pl.) | *coins* |
| la monnaie | *currency* |
| le mandat international | *international money order* |

For more vocabulary on banking, see *Banking and finance*, pages 128-30.

## Changer de l'argent *Changing money*

| | |
|---|---|
| Je voudrais encaisser un traveller. | *I would like to cash a traveller's cheque.* |
| Je voudrais changer de l'argent. | *I would like to change some money.* |
| Que dois-je faire? | *What do I have to do?* |
| Où dois-je aller? | *Where do I have to go?* |
| Où dois-je signer? | *Where do I sign?* |
| Où dois-je retirer mon argent? | *Where do I get my cash?* |
| Voilà mon passeport ma carte d'identité | *Here is my passport indentity card* |
| Comment marche le distributeur de billets? | *How do I operate the cash machine?* |
| Mon code est ... | *My PIN number is ...* |
| Je peux avoir du liquide? | *Can I get cash?* |
| J'ai combien pour ...? | *How much do I get for ...?* |
| Quel est le taux de change? | *What is the exchange rate?* |

# 14  La ville et les achats *Town and shopping*

| | |
|---|---|
| J'ai combien sur mon compte? | *How much have I got in my account?* |
| Je veux retirer de l'argent. | *I want to withdraw some money* |
| Je veux passer prendre de l'argent. | *I want to collect some money* |
| Mon nom est ... | *My name is ...* |
| J'ai perdu ma carte de crédit | *I have lost my credit card* |
| mon carnet de chèques | *cheque book* |
| mon argent | *money* |
| Que dois-je faire? | *What should I do?* |
| Comment contacter ...? | *How do I contact ...?* |
| retirer de l'argent | *to withdraw money* |
| encaisser un chèque | *to cash a cheque* |
| changer de l'argent | *to change money* |
| économiser | *to save* |
| signer | *to sign* |

## À la poste  *At the post office*

| | |
|---|---|
| le colis | *parcel* |
| le mandat { | *postal order* |
| | *money order* |
| le guichet | *counter* |
| la lettre | *letter* |
| la carte postale | *postcard* |
| les timbres | |
| (m.pl.) | *stamps* |
| l'enveloppe (f.) | *envelope* |
| le téléphone | *telephone* |
| la cabine | |
| téléphonique | *telephone box* |
| la télécarte | *telephone card* |

| | |
|---|---|
| le numéro | |
| de téléphone | *telephone number* |
| l'indicatif (m.) | *telephone code* |
| l'appel en PCV | *reverse charges call* |
| l'annuaire (m.) | *directory* |
| les renseignements | |
| (m.pl.) | *directory enquiries* |
| le combiné | *handset* |
| composer le | |
| numéro | *to dial; to tap in* |
| le loto | *lottery* |
| le numéro | *lottery number* |
| le billet de loterie | |
| | *lottery ticket* |
| le gros lot | *lottery prize* |
| la carte de | |
| grattage | *scratch card* |

| | |
|---|---|
| Je voudrais ... | *I would like ...* |
| donner (passer) un coup de téléphone | *to make a telephone call* |
| faire un appel en PCV | *to make a reverse charges call* |
| de la monnaie pour le téléphone | *change for the telephone* |
| des timbres pour une lettre | *stamps for a letter* |
| une carte postale | *a postcard* |

150

# 14 La ville et les achats *Town and shopping*

## LES DIRECTIONS *DIRECTIONS*

| | |
|---|---|
| les directions (f.pl.) | *directions* |
| à droite | *right* |
| à gauche | *left* |
| tout droit | *straight ahead* |
| | |
| Où est ...? | *Where is ...?* |
| Comment faire pour aller à la fête? | *How do I get to the fair?* |
| C'est loin? | *How far is it?* |
| C'est loin d'ici? | *Is it far from here?* |
| près d'ici? | *near here?* |
| | |
| Je peux y aller à pied? | *Can I get there on foot?* |
| Prenez la première rue à gauche | *You take the first road on the left* |
| la seconde rue à droite | *second road on the right* |
| Allez jusqu'au carrefour | *Go to the crossroads* |
| aux feux | *lights* |
| au pont | *bridge* |
| au passage à niveau | *level crossing* |
| Traversez la route | *Cross the road* |
| le pont | *bridge* |
| la ligne de chemin de fer | *railway line* |
| la place du marché | *market place* |
| Prenez le souterrain. | *Take the underpass.* |
| Quand vous arrivez à ... tournez ... | *When you come to the ... you turn ...* |
| C'est loin. | *It's far.* |
| Ce n'est pas loin. | *It's not far.* |
| C'est à cinq minutes. | *It's five minutes away.* |
| | |
| Est-ce qu'on peut y aller en bus? | *Can I get there by bus?* |
| en voiture | *car* |
| par les transports en commun | *public transport* |
| Prenez le bus numéro ... | *Take the number ... bus* |
| le métro | *underground* |
| le train | *train* |
| le tramway | *tram* |
| et descendez à ... | *and get off at ...* |
| Il y en a souvent? | *How often does it run?* |
| Toutes les (dix minutes) | *Every (ten minutes)* |
| C'est combien? | *How much does it cost?* |
| Je ne sais pas. | *I don't know.* |

151

Vous pouvez acheter une carte d'abonnement.
You can buy a multi-journey card.
Où puis-je en trouver?
Where can I get one?
à la poste
at the post office
chez le marchand de journaux
newsagent's
à la billeterie automatique
at the ticket dispenser
Vous devez annuler / valider votre billet.
You have to cancel / validate your ticket.

Une fois arrivé c'est ...
When you get there it's ...
sur la gauche / droite
on the left / right
à l'intérieur du bâtiment
inside the building
à l'extérieur de la cour
outside the courtyard
près de la fontaine
beside the fountain
au pied des escaliers
at the bottom of the steps
en face du parc
opposite the park
en haut de la colline
at the top of the hill
sur le chemin du château
on the way to the castle
face à l'église
facing the church
Vous devez aller ...
You have to go...
à gauche du musée
to the left of the museum
à droite de l'église
to the right of the church
le long de la rivière
along the river bank
Vous devez traverser le pont
You have to cross the bridge
Passez devant le monument aux morts
Go past the war memorial

| | | | |
|---|---|---|---|
| C'est ici! | *It's right here!* | prendre | *to take* |
| là-bas | *over there* | marcher | *to walk* |
| en haut | *up there* | conduire | *to drive* |
| en bas | *down there* | tourner | *to turn* |
| quelque part | *somewhere* | suivre | *to follow* |
| nulle part | *nowhere* | traverser | *to cross* |
| Je ne sais pas | *I don't know* | passer | *to pass* |
| où c'est! | *where it is!* | | |

# 15 Les voyages et le tourisme *Travel and tourism*

## LES VOYAGES
### TRAVEL

| | |
|---|---|
| l'horaire (m.) | *timetable* |
| les arrivées (f. pl.) | *arrivals* |
| les départs (m. pl.) | *departures* |
| l'excursion (f.) | *excursion* |
| la visite | *tour* |
| le voyage { | *voyage* / *journey* |

### Voyager en train
### Travel by train

| | |
|---|---|
| la gare | *station* |
| le quai | *platform* |
| le retard | *delay* |
| le passager | *passenger* |
| le billet | *ticket* |
| l'aller simple (m.) | *single ticket* |
| l'aller-retour (m.) | *return ticket* |
| le billet à tarif réduit } | *cheap ticket* / *super saver* |
| le demi-tarif | *half fare* |
| le plein tarif | *full fare* |
| le distributeur automatique | *machine to issue, cancel and date-stamp ticket* |
| la billeterie automatique | *automatic ticket machine* |
| le TGV (le train à grande vitesse) | *TGV (high-speed train)* |

| | |
|---|---|
| le rapide } le corail } | *Inter-city express* |
| l'express | *fast train* |
| le train auto-couchettes | *motorail* |
| l'omnibus (m.) | *slow train* |
| les marchandises (f. pl.) | *freight* |
| un TER | *local train* |

| | |
|---|---|
| électrique | *electric* |
| diesel | *diesel* |
| à vapeur | *steam* |

| | |
|---|---|
| le wagon-restaurant | *restaurant car* |
| le train couchettes | *sleeper* |
| la couchette | *couchette* |
| le bar | *buffet car* |
| le compartiment | *railway carriage* |
| le moteur | *engine* |
| les signaux (m. pl.) | *signals* |
| l'aiguillage (m.) | *points* |
| les rails (m. pl.) | *rails* |
| la ligne | *line* |
| les lignes à haute tension (f. pl.) | *overhead cables* |

FUMEUR
*SMOKING*

NON FUMEUR
*NON SMOKING*

---

| | |
|---|---|
| Il faut réserver en avance? | *Do you have to book in advance?* |
| A quelle heure part le train? | *What time does the train leave?* |
| Quel quai? | *What platform?* |
| C'est direct? | *Do I have to change?* |
| C'est le train pour ...? | *Is this the train for ...?* |

# 15 Les voyages et le tourisme *Travel and tourism*

| | |
|---|---|
| réserver | *to book in advance* |
| réserver une place | *to reserve a seat* |
| voyager sans billet | *to travel without a ticket* |
| composter | *to validate a ticket* |

## Voyager en avion
### *Travel by plane*

| | |
|---|---|
| l'aéroport (m.) | *airport* |
| les arrivées (f. pl.) | *arrivals* |
| les départs (m. pl.) | *departures* |
| la salle d'embarquement | *departure lounge* |
| la carte d'accès à bord | *boarding card* |
| la classe affaire | *business class* |
| l'enregistrement (m.) | *check-in (desk)* |
| le douanier | *customs officer* |
| la classe économique | *economy class* |
| la première classe | *first class* |
| le vol | *flight* |
| la porte | *gate* |
| allez au comptoir ... | *go to desk ...* |
| à la porte ... | *go to gate ...* |
| l'immigration (f.) | *immigration* |
| la carte d'immigration | *immigration form* |
| le carrousel | *luggage carousel* |
| l'étiquette | *luggage label* |
| | |
| le trou d'air | *air pocket* |
| l'allée (f.) | *aisle* |
| le couloir | *corridor* |

| | |
|---|---|
| la cabine | *cabin* |
| le steward en chef | *chief steward* |
| le steward | *steward* |
| l'hôtesse de l'air (f.) | *stewardess* |
| la catastrophe aérienne | *plane crash* |
| l'équipage (m.) | *crew* |
| la porte | *door* |
| la sortie de secours | *emergency exit* |
| le problème de moteur | *engine trouble* |
| le fuselage | *fuselage* |
| le casque ⎫ les écouteurs ⎬ (m. pl.) ⎭ | *headset* |
| le jet | *jet* |
| l'atterrissage (m.) | *landing* |
| le gilet de sauvetage | *life jacket* |
| le chargement | *loading* |
| le bagage | *luggage* |
| le navigateur | *navigator* |
| le numéro de siège | *seat number* |
| le passeport | *passport* |
| le contrôle des passeports | *passport control* |
| le pilote | *pilot* |
| la file d'attente | *queue* |
| la rangée | *row* |
| la piste | *runway* |
| la ceinture de sécurité (f. pl.) | *safety belt* |
| les consignes de sécurité (f. pl.) | *safety regulations* |
| la place | *seat* |
| le co-pilote | *second pilot* |
| la passerelle | *stairs* |

# 15 Les voyages et le tourisme *Travel and tourism*

| | | | |
|---|---|---|---|
| les marches | | le car | coach |
| (f. pl.) | steps | la gare routière | bus station |
| la tablette | fold-down table | l'arrêt de bus (m.) | bus stop |
| la queue | tail | le prix du ticket | fare |
| les turbulences | | le chauffeur ⎫ | driver |
| (f. pl.) | turbulence | le conducteur ⎭ | |
| en haut | upstairs | le steward | steward |
| la sortie | way out | l'hôtesse | stewardess |
| le siège côté | | le siège | seat |
| hublot | window seat | le couloir | aisle |
| l'aile (f.) | wing | | |

| | |
|---|---|
| atterrir | to land |
| décoller | to take off |
| faire la queue | to queue |

## Voyager en bateau
### *Travel by boat*

| | |
|---|---|
| le pont | deck |
| le ferry | ferry |
| la passerelle de ⎧ | gang plank |
| débarquement ⎩ | ramp |
| le commissaire | |
| de bord | purser |
| les portes d'embarquement | |
| des véhicules | |
| (f. pl.) | vehicle loading doors |
| la croisière | cruise |
| le commandant | |
| du navire | ship's captain |
| la mer est ... | the sea is ... |
| mauvaise | rough |
| calme | smooth |
| naviguer | to sail |
| avoir le mal | |
| de mer | to be seasick |
| accoster | to dock |

## Voyager en bus
### *Travel by bus*

| | |
|---|---|
| le bus | bus |

## Voyager en tramway
### *Travel by tram*

| | |
|---|---|
| le tram | tram |
| l'arrêt de tram | |
| (m.) | tram stop |
| la ligne de tram | tramline |
| le conducteur | driver |
| le distributeur | |
| de tickets | ticket machine |

## Voyager en vélo *Travel by bike*

(See also *Hobbies and sports*,
page 114)

| | |
|---|---|
| le vélo ⎫ | bicycle |
| la bicyclette ⎭ | |
| le VTT | mountain bike |
| (le vélo tout terrain) | |
| la moto | motorbike |
| le scooter | scooter |
| le guidon | handlebars |
| les roues (f. pl.) | wheels |
| les pneus (m. pl.) | tyres |
| le pneu crevé | puncture |
| les freins | |
| (m. pl.) | brakes |
| la pompe | pump |
| la trousse de | |
| réparation | repair kit |
| la chaîne | chain |

# 15 Les voyages et le tourisme *Travel and tourism*

## LE TOURISME
### *TOURISM*

| | |
|---|---|
| l'agence de voyage (f.) | *travel agent* |
| la brochure | *brochure* |
| la fiche de réservation | *booking form* |
| le billet | *ticket* |
| l'assurance (f.) | *insurance* |
| le visa | *visa* |
| les vaccinations (f. pl.) | { *jabs* *inoculations* |
| | |
| le parc à thème | *theme park* |
| l'endroit sauvage (m.) | *area of natural beauty* |

| | |
|---|---|
| le parc national | *national park* |
| la Côte d'Azur | *the Riviera* |
| la station de ski | *ski resort* |
| la station balnéaire | *seaside resort* |
| | |
| Je veux visiter. | *I want to see the sights.* |
| l'abbaye (f.) | *abbey* |
| le monument historique | *ancient monument* |
| le lieu de naissance | *birthplace* |
| le pont | *bridge* |
| le château | *castle* |
| la cathédrale | *cathedral* |

| | |
|---|---|
| J'aime passer mes vacances ... | *I like to spend my holidays ...* |
| en ville | *in a city* |
| à la campagne | *in the country* |
| à la montagne | *in the mountains* |
| au bord de la mer | *at the seaside* |
| à la maison | *at home* |
| en mer | *at sea* |
| | |
| Je préfère des vacances ... | *I prefer ...* |
| loin de tout | *a holiday away from it all* |
| à ne rien faire | *a lazy holiday* |
| à l'étranger | *an overseas holiday* |
| au bord de la mer | *a sea, sun, sand holiday* |
| sportives | *an active holiday* |
| | |
| la station de vacances | *holiday resort* |
| le voyage | *trip* |
| le voyage organisé | *tour* |
| la croisière | *cruise* |
| partir le sac au dos | *back packing* |
| faire de la marche | *walking holiday* |
| partir en week-end | *weekend holiday* |
| l'excursion d'une journée (f.) | *day trip* |
| les vacances actives | *activity holiday* |
| les vacances avec mes copains | *holiday with my mates* |

# 15 Les voyages et le tourisme *Travel and tourism*

| | |
|---|---|
| la grotte | *cave* |
| l'église (f.) | *church* |
| la forêt | *forest* |
| les gorges (f. pl.) | *gorge* |
| le monument historique | *historic building* |
| le lac | *lake* |
| le monument | *monument* |
| la montagne | *mountain* |
| le musée | *museum* |
| la rivière | *river* |
| romain(e) | *Roman* |
| maure, mauresque | *Moorish* |
| la mer | *sea* |
| le château ⎫<br>le domaine ⎭ | *stately home* |
| la vue | *view* |
| | |
| le/la touriste | *the tourist* |
| le visiteur | *visitor* |
| le voyageur | *traveller* |
| le randonneur | *backpacker* |
| le vacancier | *holidaymaker* |
| les fort en gueule | *lager louts* |
| l'après-soleil (m.) | *after-sun cream* |
| la banane | *bum bag* |
| l'appareil photo (m.) | *camera* |
| l'adaptateur (m.) | *electric adaptor* |

| | |
|---|---|
| le guide | { *guide*<br>{ *guide book* |
| la carte | *map* |
| la ceinture pour l'argent | *money belt* |
| l'anti-moustiques (m.) | *mosquito repellent* |
| le passeport | *passport* |
| le manuel de vocabulaire | *phrase book* |
| le sac à dos | *rucksack* |
| le souvenir | *souvenir* |
| la valise | *suitcase* |
| la crème solaire | *sun cream* |
| la lotion | *lotion* |
| le plan de la ville | *town plan* |
| le guide de voyage | *travel guide* |
| les chaussures de marche (f. pl.) | *walking boots* |
| réserver | *to book* |
| acheter | *to buy* |
| visiter | *to visit* |
| prendre en photo | *to photograph* |
| filmer | *to film* |
| voyager | *to travel* |
| partir à l'étranger | *to go abroad* |
| rester | *to stay* |

## LE LOGEMENT EN VACANCES
### *HOLIDAY ACCOMMODATION*

| Nous allons rester ... | *We are going to stay ...* |
|---|---|

# Camping de Brallac'h ★★
## Mousterlin

| au camping | *on a campsite* |
|---|---|
| l'hôtel | *in a hotel* |
| dans un foyer | *in a hostel* |
| dans une pension | *at a guest house* |
| dans une chambre d'hôte | *in a bed and breakfast* |
| dans une auberge | *at an inn* |
| dans une ferme | *on a farm* |
| dans une maison familiale | *in a holiday home* |
| dans un camp de vacances | *in a holiday park* |
| dans une auberge de jeunesse | *in a youth hostel* |

### À l'hôtel *In the hotel*

| la réception | *reception* |
|---|---|
| le bar | *bar* |
| le restaurant | *restaurant* / *dining room* |
| le salon | *lounge* |
| la boutique | *shop* |
| les escaliers (m. pl.) | *stairs* |
| l'ascenseur (m.) | *lift* |
| la piscine | *swimming pool* |
| la salle de gym | *fitness room* |
| les vestiaires (m. pl.) | *changing rooms* |

| la chambre | *room* |
|---|---|
| la chambre double | *double bed room* |
| la chambre simple | *single room* |
| avec douche | *with shower* |
| bain | *bath* |
| télé | *TV* |
| téléphone | *phone* |
| balcon | *balcony* |
| vue sur la mer | *sea view* |

158

# 15 Les voyages et le tourisme *Travel and tourism*

## Au camping *On a campsite*

| | |
|---|---|
| le camping car | *camper van* |
| la caravane | *caravan* |
| l'électricité (f.) | *electricity* |
| le parking | *parking* |
| les poubelles (f. pl.) | *refuse* |
| les douches (f. pl.) | *showers* |
| les lavabos (m. pl.) | *sinks* |
| l'emplacement (m.) | *site* |
| la tente | *tent* |
| les toilettes (f. pl.) | *toilets* |
| les sanitaires (m. pl.) | *washing facilities* |
| l'eau (f.) | *water* |

## À l'auberge de jeunesse *In the youth hostel*

| | |
|---|---|
| la salle à manger | *dining room* |
| le dortoir | *dormitory* |
| la cuisine | *kitchen* |
| la salle de jeux | *recreation room* |
| le règlement | *regulations* |
| les toilettes (f. pl.) | *toilets* |
| le / la gardien (-ienne) | *warden* |

---

## *ENCORE!*

● *Activity: Fill in the form.*

### Hôtel Jeanne d'Arc
### FICHE D'ACCEUIL

Nom (*name*) _____

Domicile (*place of residence*) _____

Lieu de naissance (*place of birth*) _____

Date de naissance (*date of birth*) _____

Nationalité (*nationality*) _____

Numéro d'immatriculation (*car registration no.*) _____

Date d'arrivée (*date of arrival*) _____

Date de départ (*date of departure*) _____

Numéro de passeport/carte d'identité (*identity card/passport*) _____

## 15 Les voyages et le tourisme *Travel and tourism*

### AU BORD DE LA MER
### *AT THE SEASIDE*

| | |
|---|---|
| la mer | sea |
| les falaises (f. pl.) | cliffs |
| l'île (f.) | island |
| les rochers (m. pl.) | rocks |
| le port | port |
| le dock | dock |
| le phare | lighthouse |
| la bouée | buoy |
| le bateau | boat |
| le navire | ship |
| le voilier | sailing ship |
| le bateau à vapeur | steam ship |
| le bateau de pêche | fishing boat |
| le chalutier | trawler |
| le bateau à moteur | motor boat |
| le sous-marin | submarine |
| le ferry | ferry |
| le paquebot | cruise liner |
| le bateau de débarquement | Roll-on-roll-off ferry |
| le porte-conteneurs | container ship |
| | |
| la cheminée | funnel |
| le moteur | engine |
| l'ancre (f.) | anchor |
| les voiles (f. pl.) | sails |
| le pont | bridge |
| la cabine | cabin |
| les portes des cales (f. pl.) | freight doors |
| le radar | radar |
| la proue | bow |
| la poupe | stern |
| bâbord et tribord | port and starboard |

| | |
|---|---|
| le vent fort | gale |
| le brouillard | fog |

(See also *Weather and the climate*, pages 172–3.)

| | |
|---|---|
| la corne de brume | fog horn |
| le capitaine | captain |
| le marin | sailor |
| l'équipage (m.) | crew |
| le commissaire de bord | purser |
| le navigateur | navigator |
| | |
| la noyade | drowning |
| l'embarcation (f.) | embarcation |
| l'iceberg (m.) | iceberg |
| le gilet de sauvetage | lifebelt |
| le radeau de sauvetage | lifeboat |
| le naufrage | shipwreck |
| appareiller | { to set sail / to cast off } |
| manœuvrer | to steer |
| écoper | to bail out |
| | |
| faire naufrage | to be shipwrecked |
| se noyer | to drown |
| heurter une roche | to hit a rock |
| sauver, porter secours | to rescue |
| sombrer/couler | to sink |
| nager | to swim |

### Sur la plage *On the beach*

| | |
|---|---|
| la plage | the beach |
| le sable | sand |
| la dune | dune |
| l'algue (f.) | seaweed |

# 15 Les voyages et le tourisme *Travel and tourism*

| | |
|---|---|
| la mer | *sea* |
| la marée | *tide* |
| la marée haute | *high tide* |
| la marée basse | *low tide* |
| le galet | *shingle* |
| le transat | *deck chair* |
| le pare-vent | *wind breaker* |
| le seau et la pelle | *bucket and spade* |
| le pique-nique | *picnic* |
| le marchand de glaces | *ice-cream kiosk* |
| la serviette | *towel* |
| le maillot | *swimming costume* |

(See also *Clothes and fashion*, page 54)

| | |
|---|---|
| la crème solaire | *sun cream* |
| la lotion apaisante | *sunburn lotion* |

| | |
|---|---|
| la crème après-soleil | *after-sun cream* |
| les lunettes de soleil (f. pl.) | *sun glasses* |
| le sable entre les orteils | *sand between the toes* |
| les palmes (f. pl.) | *flippers* |
| le tuba | *snorkel* |

(See also *Hobbies and sports*, pages 114–15)

| | |
|---|---|
| creuser | *to dig* |
| se bronzer | *to sunbathe* |
| nager | *to swim* |
| se détendre | *to relax* |
| faire des châteaux de sable | *to build sandcastles* |

# 15 Les voyages et le tourisme *Travel and tourism*

## LA VOITURE
### *CARS AND MOTORING*

| | |
|---|---|
| l'accident (m.) | *accident* |
| la route | *road* |
| les panneaux (m. pl.) | *road signs* |
| la station service | *petrol station services* |

## Les pièces détachées et les accessoires *Car parts and accessories*

| | |
|---|---|
| les accessoires (m. pl.) | *accessories* |
| la voiture | *car* |
| la carrosserie | *body* |
| le freinage ABS | *ABS braking* |
| le capot | *bonnet* |
| le coffre | *boot* |
| les freins (m. pl.) | *brakes* |
| le pare-chocs | *bumper* |
| le pot catalytique | *catalytic converter* |
| le chassis | *chassis* |
| l'embrayage (m.) | *clutch* |
| la portière | *door* |
| le moteur | *engine* |
| l'échappement (m.) | *exhaust* |
| la vitesse | *gear* |
| la boîte de vitesse | *gear box* |
| les phares (m. pl.) | *headlamps* |
| les clignotants (m. pl.) | *indicators* |
| les pièces (f. pl.) | *parts* |
| la direction assistée | *power-assisted steering* |

| | |
|---|---|
| le réservoir | *petrol tank* |
| le bouchon du réservoir | *petrol cap* |
| le toit | *roof* |
| les sièges (m. pl.) | *seats* |
| les feux de position | *side lights* |
| le volant | *steering wheel* |
| le pneu | *tyre* |
| la roue | *wheel* |
| la vitre | *window* |
| les essuie-glace (m. pl.) | *windscreen wipers* |
| l'aile (f.) | *wing* |

| | |
|---|---|
| la voiture automatique | *automatic* |
| la voiture de sport | *sports car* |
| la Formule 1 (Un) | *formula 1* |
| le coupé | *hatchback* |
| le quatre-quatre | *four-wheel drive* |
| les performances (f. pl.) | *performance* |
| la vitesse | *speed* |
| le freinage | *braking* |
| la direction | *steering* |
| la puissance | *horse power* |
| le lavojet | *car wash (machine)* |
| le lave-vitre | *screen wash* |
| le polish | *car wax* |

| | |
|---|---|
| l'auto-école (f.) | *driving school* |
| l'assurance (f.) | *insurance* |
| le jeune conducteur | *learner* or *recently passed driver* |
| le permis de conduire | *licence* |
| le manuel d'utilisation | *manual* |

# 15  Les voyages et le tourisme *Travel and tourism*

| | | | |
|---|---|---|---|
| le contrôle technique | *MOT* | la route communale | *country road* |
| le permis provisoire | *provisional licence* | le sens unique | *one-way street* |
| | | l'impasse (f.) | *cul de sac* |
| l'accident (m.) | *accident* | l'aquaplaning (m.) | *aquaplaning* |
| l'aide (f.) | *assistance* | les virages (m. pl.) | *bends* |
| l'automobile club (m.) | *Automobile Association (equivalent)* | la déviation | *diversion* |
| la panne | *breakdown* | les warnings | *emergency lights* |
| le dépannage | *breakdown assistance* | la bande d'arrêt d'urgence | *hard shoulder* |
| la collision | *collision* | les vents forts (m. pl.) | *high winds* |
| la barre anti-vol | *crooklok* | | |
| le bouchon / l'embouteillage | *traffic jam* | la voie | *lane* |
| le carambolage | *pile-up* | ne pas dépasser | *no overtaking* |
| la crevaison | *puncture* | la voie de dépassement | *overtaking lane* |
| la réparation | *repair* | les travaux (m. pl.) | *road works* |

## Les routes et la signalisation
### *Roads and road signs*

| | | | |
|---|---|---|---|
| | | la borne d'appel | *roadside phone* |
| l'autoroute (f.) | *motorway* | la route à double sens | *single carriageway / two-way traffic* |
| la double voie | *dual carriageway* | la limitation de vitesse | *speed restriction* |
| la nationale | *A-road* | les feux (m. pl.) | *traffic lights* |
| la départementale | *B-road* | le bas-côté | *verge* |

## À la station service
### *At the services*

| | |
|---|---|
| la station service | *petrol station* |
| la pompe à essence | *petrol pump* |
| l'essence (f.) | *petrol* |
| le super | *four-star petrol* |
| le sans plomb | *unleaded petrol* |
| le gasoil | *diesel* |
| l'huile (f.) | *oil* |
| la pression des pneus | *tyre pressure* |
| la carte routière | *road map* |

# 15 Les voyages et le tourisme *Travel and tourism*

| | |
|---|---|
| le triangle de présignalisation | *warning triangle* |
| l'ampoule (f.) | *light bulb* |
| le déflecteur de phare | *headlamp deflector* |
| le liquide de frein | *brake fluid* |
| l'anti-gel (m.) | *anti-freeze* |
| le lave-vitre | *windscreen wash* |
| le shampooing auto | *car wash* |

| | | | | |
|---|---|---|---|---|
| l'assurance (f.) | *insurance* | heurter | *to hit* |
| la carte verte | *green card* | perdre le | |
| les papiers | | contrôle | *to lose control* |
| (m. pl.) | *car documents* | dépasser | *to overtake* |
| | | faire marche | |
| freiner | *to brake* | arrière | *to reverse* |
| tomber en | | écraser | *to run over* |
| panne | *to break down* | déraper | *to skid* |
| changer de | | accéléler | *to speed* |
| vitesse | *to change gear* | conduire | *to steer* |
| emboutir | *to collide* | faire un écart | *to swerve* |
| conduire | *to drive* | | |

# 16 La nature *The natural world*

## LA CAMPAGNE
### *THE COUNTRYSIDE*

| | |
|---|---|
| le paysage | *landscape* |
| le pays | *country* |
| le village | *village* |
| l'église (f.) | *church* |
| le ruisseau | *stream* |
| la rivière | *river* |
| la chute d'eau | *waterfall* |
| les rochers (m. pl.) | *rocks* |
| le lac | *lake* |
| la piscine naturelle | *rock pool* |
| la mare | *pond* |
| l'étang (m.) | { *small lake* / *pond* } |
| le marais | *marsh* |
| la plaine | *plain* |
| la vallée | *valley* |
| le désert | *desert* |
| la colline | *hill* |
| la montagne | *mountain* |
| la chaîne de montagnes | *mountain range* |
| le pic montagneux | *mountain peak* |
| le sommet | *summit* |
| le funiculaire | *funicular* |
| le téléphérique | *cable railway* |
| le champ | *field* |
| la prairie | *grassland* |
| le portail | *gate* |
| la clôture | { *wall* / *fence* } |
| la haie | *hedge* |

| | |
|---|---|
| le sentier | *path* |
| l'échalier (m.) | *stile* |
| le chemin piétonnier | *footpath* |
| le bois | *wood* |
| la forêt | *forest* |
| l'arbre (m.) | *tree* |
| le conifère | *coniferous tree* |
| l'arbre à feuilles caduques | *deciduous tree* |
| le frêne | *ash* |
| le hêtre (m.) | *beech* |
| le sapin | *fir* |
| le houx | *holly* |
| l'érable (m.) | *maple* |
| le chêne | *oak* |
| le pin | *pine* |
| le platane | *plane* |
| le peuplier | *poplar* |
| le bouleau argenté | *silver birch* |
| le sycomore | *sycamore* |
| le saule | *willow* |
| le saule pleureur | *weeping willow* |
| le mélèze | *larch* |
| marcher | *to walk* |
| faire de la randonnée | *to hike* |
| faire du vélo | *to cycle* |
| faire du cheval | *to ride* |
| faire un pique-nique | *to picnic* |
| faire un footing | *to go for a run* |

# 16 La nature *The natural world*

## ENCORE!

● *Activity: What do the symbols mean?*

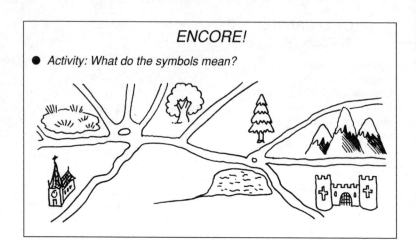

# 16 La nature *The natural world*

## À LA FERME
### ON THE FARM

| | |
|---|---|
| la ferme | *farm* |
| les bâtiments de ferme (m.pl.) | *farm buildings* |
| la cour de ferme | *farm yard* |
| la chaumière | *cottage* |
| la terre cultivable | *arable land* |
| le bétail | *cattle* |
| les produits laitiers (m.pl.) | *dairy products* |
| le bœuf | *beef* |
| la grange | *barn* |
| l'étable (f.) | { *cowshed* / *byre* |
| la remise | *shed* |
| l'écurie (f.) | *stable* |

## Les animaux de la ferme
### Farm animals

| | |
|---|---|
| la vache | *cow* |
| le taureau | *bull* |
| le veau | *calf* |
| le cheval | *horse* |
| l'étalon (m.) | *stallion* |
| la jument | *mare* |
| le poulain | *foal* (horse) |
| l'âne (m.) | *donkey* |
| l'ânon (m.) | *foal* (donkey) |
| la mule | *mule* |
| le cheval de trait | *cart horse* |
| le poney | *pony* |
| le mouton | *sheep* |
| le bélier | *ram* |
| l'agneau (m.) | *lamb* |
| le cochon | *pig* |
| la truie | *sow* |
| le verrat | *boar* |

| | |
|---|---|
| le porcelet | *piglet* |
| la chèvre | *goat* |
| le bouc | *billy goat* |
| la biquette | *nanny goat* |
| le chevreau | *kid* |
| la poule | *hen* |
| le poulet | *chicken* |
| le coq | *cockerel* |
| le poussin | *chick* |
| l'œuf | *egg* |
| l'oie (f.) | *goose* |
| le jars | *gander* |
| l'oison (m.) | *gosling* |
| le canard | *duck (drake)* |
| la cane | *female duck* |
| le caneton | *duckling* |
| le tracteur | *tractor* |
| la charrue | *plough* |
| la moissonneuse | *harvester* |
| le maïs | *corn* |
| le grain | *grain* |
| l'avoine (f.) | *oats* |
| le blé | *wheat* |
| l'orge (f.) | *barley* |
| le seigle | *rye* |
| la prairie | *grassland* |
| le foin | *hay* |
| la paille | *straw* |
| la palissade | *fence* |
| la barrière | *farm gate* |
| la haie | *hedge* |
| l'enclos (m.) | *paddock* |
| semer/planter | *to sow/plant* |
| cultiver | *to cultivate, to grow* |
| nourrir les animaux | *to feed animals* |
| moissonner | *to harvest* |
| passer la moissonneuse-batteuse | *to combine harvest* |
| irriguer | *to irrigate* |

# 16 La nature *The natural world*

## LES ANIMAUX SAUVAGES
### *WILD ANIMALS*

| | |
|---|---|
| le blaireau | *badger* |
| le furet | *ferret* |
| le renard | *fox* |
| la grenouille | *frog* |
| le lièvre | *hare* |
| le hérisson | *hedgehog* |
| le vison | *mink* |
| la taupe | *mole* |
| la souris | *mouse* |
| la loutre | *otter* |
| le rat | *rat* |
| l'écureuil (m.) | *squirrel* |
| le crapaud | *toad* |
| la belette | *weasel* |
| le ver de terre | *worm* |

### En safari *On safari*

| | |
|---|---|
| l'antilope (f.) | *antelope* |
| le bison | *bison* |
| l'ours brun (m.) | *brown bear* |
| le buffle | *buffalo* |
| le chameau | *camel* |
| le dauphin | *dolphin* |
| l'éléphant (m.) | *elephant* |
| l'élan (m.) | *elk* |
| la girafe | *giraffe* |
| le grizzly | *grizzly bear* |
| l'hippopotame (m.) | *hippopotamus* |
| la hyène (f.) | *hyena* |
| le jaguar | *jaguar* |
| le kangourou | *kangaroo* |
| le koala | *koala* |
| le léopard | *leopard* |
| le lion | *lion* |
| le singe | *monkey* |
| l'élan (m.) | *moose* |
| la panthère | *panther* |
| le renne | *reindeer* |
| le rhinocéros | *rhinoceros* |

| | |
|---|---|
| le phoque | *seal* |
| la moufette | *skunk* |
| le serpent | *snake* |
| le tigre | *tiger* |
| la baleine | *whale* |
| le sanglier | *wild boar* |
| le loup | *wolf* |
| le zèbre | *zebra* |

## Le corps de l'animal
### *Parts of the animal*

| | |
|---|---|
| les bois (m.pl.) | *antlers* |
| les griffes (f.pl.) | *claws* |
| le pelage | *coat* |
| la fourrure | *fur* |
| le poil | *hair* |
| le sabot | *hoof* |
| la corne | *horn* |
| la patte | *paw* |
| l'écaille (f.) | *scale* |
| la coquille | *shell* |
| la peau | *skin* |
| la queue | *tail* |
| la trompe | *trunk* |
| la défense | *tusk* |

## Les oiseaux *Birds*

| | |
|---|---|
| oberver les oiseaux | *bird watching* |
| le merle | *blackbird* |
| la mésange | *blue-tit* |
| la buse | *buzzard* |
| le pinson | *chaffinch* |
| le cormoran | *cormorant* |
| le corbeau | *crow* |
| le coucou | *cuckoo* |
| la colombe | *dove* |
| l'aigle (m.) | *eagle* |
| le coq de bruyère | *grouse* |
| le faucon | *hawk* |

# 16 La nature *The natural world*

| | |
|---|---|
| le martin pêcheur | *kingfisher* |
| la pie | *magpie* |
| le martinet | *martin* |
| le rossignol | *nightingale* |
| l'aigrette (f.) | *osprey* |
| le hibou | *(barn) owl* |
| la perdrix | *partridge* |
| le pélican | *pelican* |
| le faisan | *pheasant* |
| le pigeon | *pigeon* |
| le rouge-gorge | *robin* |
| le freux | *rook* |
| la mouette | *seagull* |
| l'alouette (f.) | *skylark* |
| la bécasse | *snipe* |
| le moineau | *sparrow* |
| l'étourneau (m.) | *starling* |
| la cigogne | *stork* |
| l'hirondelle (f.) | *swallow* |
| le cygne | *swan* |
| le martinet | *swift* |
| la grive | *thrush* |
| le vautour | *vulture* |
| le bec | *beak* |
| la griffe | *claw* |
| l'œuf (m.) | *egg* |
| la plume | *feather* |
| le nid | *nest* |
| l'aile (f.) | *wing* |

## Les insectes *Insects*

| | |
|---|---|
| la fourmi | *ant* |
| l'abeille (f.) | *bee* |
| la ruche | *bee-hive* |
| le nid d'abeilles | *honeycomb* |
| le miel | *honey* |
| la mouche bleue | *bluebottle* |
| le papillon | *butterfly* |

| | |
|---|---|
| la chenille | *caterpillar* |
| le cafard | *cockroach* |
| la libellule | *dragonfly* |
| la puce | *flea* |
| la mouche | *fly* |
| la sauterelle | *grasshopper* |
| la larve | *grub* |
| le taon | *horse fly* |
| la coccinelle | *ladybird* |
| le moucheron | *midge* |
| le moustique | *mosquito* |
| le papillon de nuit | *moth* |
| l'araignée (f.) | *spider* |
| la toile d'araignée | *spider's web* |
| l'insecte qui pique | *stinging insect* |
| la guêpe | *wasp* |
| le nid de guêpes | *wasp's nest* |

## Soyez prêts! *Be prepared!*

| | |
|---|---|
| la crème antihistaminique | *antihistamine cream* |
| les jumelles (f.pl.) | *binoculars* |
| la piqûre de (moustique) | *(mosquito) bite* |
| l'appareil photo (m.) | *camera* |
| l'insecticide (m.) | *fly pray* |
| la cachette d'observation | *hide* |
| les cachets contre la malaria (m.pl.) | *malaria tablets* |
| la moustiquaire | *mosquito net* |
| la piqûre (d'abeille) | *(bee) sting* |

# 16 La nature *The natural world*

| | | | | |
|---|---|---|---|---|
| la corrida | *bullfight* | ramper | *to crawl* |
| la chasse | { *hunt* / *hunting* | chanter | *to crow* |
| | | grogner | *to grunt* |
| chasser | *to hunt* | siffler | *to hiss* |
| le tir | { *shoot* / *shooting* | huhuler | *to hoot* |
| | | hurler | *to howl* |
| tirer | *to shoot* | chasser | *to hunt* |
| | | miauler | *to maiow* |
| aboyer | *to bark* | mugir | *to moo* |
| beugler | *to bellow* | hennir | *to neigh* |
| piquer | *to bite* | ronronner | *to purr* |
| bêler | *to bleat* | rugir | *to roar* |
| bourdonner | *to buzz* | piquer | *to sting* |
| attraper | *to catch* | barrir | *to trumpet* |

# 16 La nature *The natural world*

## LES PROBLÈMES D'ENVIRONNEMENT
### *ENVIRONMENTAL ISSUES*

| | |
|---|---|
| l'environnement (m.) | *environment* |
| la pollution | *environmental pollution* |
| le recyclage | *re-cycling* |
| la pluie acide | *acid rain* |
| la forêt équatoriale | *rain forest* |
| le désert | *desert* |
| la pollution de l'eau | *water pollution* |
| la pollution de l'air | *air pollution* |
| la couche d'ozone | *ozone layer* |
| la protection de l'environnement | *environmental protection* |
| le CFC | *CFC* |
| la surpopulation | *overpopulation* |
| le défrichement | *land reclamation* |
| la destruction de l'habitat naturel | *destruction of the habitat* |
| ... de la forêt équatoriale | *of the rain forest ...* |
| de l'environnement ... | *... of the environment* |
| l'érosion du sol (f.) | *soil erosion* |
| la centrale électrique | *power station* |
| le carburant | *fuel* |
| l'essence (f.) | *petrol* |
| le gaz | *gas* |
| le charbon | *coal* |
| le pétrole | *(petroleum) crude oil* |
| solide | *solid* |
| l'énergie nucléaire (f.) | *nuclear power* |
| le combustible nucléaire | *nuclear fuel* |
| la station nucléaire | *nuclear power station* |
| la fusion nucléaire | *nuclear fusion* |
| la radiation | *radiation* |
| l'énergie hydro-électrique | *hydoelectric power* |
| l'énergie solaire (f.) | *solar power* |
| la protection des animaux | *protection of animals* |

# 16 La nature *The natural world*

## LE TEMPS ET LE CLIMAT
### *WEATHER AND THE CLIMATE*

| | |
|---|---|
| le temps | *the weather* |
| l'air (m.) | *air* |
| l'atmosphère (f.) | *atmosphere* |
| le baromètre | *barometer* |
| le climat | *climate* |
| le froid | *cold* |
| la sécheresse | *drought* |
| les prévisions (f.pl.) | *forecast* |
| la chaleur | *heat* |
| l'humidité (f.) | *humidity* |
| la chute de pluie | *rainfall* |
| le ciel | *sky* |
| le thermomètre | *thermometer* |
| la visibilité | *visibility* |
| | |
| le mauvais temps | *bad weather* |
| les éclaircies (f.pl.) | *bright intervals* |
| la brise | *breeze* |
| le nuage | *cloud* |
| la rosée | *dew* |
| le déluge | *downpour* |
| l'inondation (f.) | *flood* |
| le brouillard | *fog* |
| la rafale | *gust* |
| la grêle | *hail* |
| la vague de chaleur | *heat wave* |
| le verglas | *(black) ice* |
| le glaçon | *icicle* |
| la brume | *mist* |
| la mousson | *monsoon* |
| la pluie | *rain* |
| l'arc-en-ciel (m.) | *rainbow* |
| l'averse (f.) | *shower* |

| | |
|---|---|
| la neige fondue | *sleet* |
| la neige | *snow* |
| la boule de neige | *snowball* |
| le bonhomme de neige | *snowman* |
| le chasse-neige | *snowplough* |
| la tempête de neige | *snowstorm* |
| le soleil | *sun* |
| la tempête / l'orage (m.) | *storm* |
| le tonnerre et les éclairs (m.pl.) | *thunder and lightning* |
| la tornade | *whirlwind* |
| le vent | *wind* |
| le vent du nord | *north wind* |
| le vent du sud | *south wind* |
| le vent du sud-est | *south-easterly wind* |
| | |
| Le temps est ... | *The weather is ....* |
| changeant | *changeable* |
| froid | *cold* |
| frais | *cool* |
| sec | *dry* |
| beau | *fine* |
| brumeux | *foggy* |
| lourd | *heavy* |
| chaud | *hot* |
| lourd | *humid* |
| doux | *mild* |
| pluvieux | *rainy / wet* |
| orageux | *stormy* |
| | |
| le ciel est ... | *The sky is ...* |
| bleu | *blue* |
| dégagé | *clear* |
| nuageux | *cloudy* |
| sombre | *dark* |
| couvert | *heavy / overcast* |

# 16 La nature *The natural world*

| | | | |
|---|---|---|---|
| changer | *to change* | dégeler | *to thaw* |
| se lever | *to clear up* | | |
| geler | *to freeze* | C'est ... | *It's ...* |
| grêler | *to hail* | C'était ... | *It was ...* |
| s'améliorer | *to improve* | nuageux | *cloudy* |
| fondre | *to melt* | froid | *cold* |
| pleuvoir | *to rain* | brumeux | *foggy* |
| briller | *to shine* | glacial | *freezing* |
| neiger | *to snow* | | |

| | |
|---|---|
| Il grêle | *It's hailing* |
| Il fait très chaud | *very hot* |
| Il fait chaud | *hot* |
|     lourd | *humid* |
| | |
| Il y a du tonnerre et des éclairs | *There's thunder and lightning* |
| Il y a du vent | *It's windy* |
| Il pleut | *raining* |
| Il neige | *snowing* |
| Il y aura des averses | *There will be showers* |
|     des éclaircies (f.pl.) | *bright intervals* |
|     des vents forts (m.pl.) | *strong winds* |
|     de la neige | *snow* |

## 17 Le vaste monde *The wider world*

### LE MONDE
### *THE WORLD*

| | |
|---|---|
| la terre | *the earth* |
| le globe | *the globe* |
| l'équateur (m.) | *equator* |
| les tropiques (m.pl.) | *the tropics* |
| le tropique du Capricorne | *Tropic of Capricorn* |
| le tropique du Cancer | *Tropic of Cancer* |
| le cercle polaire arctique | *Arctic Circle* |
| l'océan Arctique (m.) | *Arctic Ocean* |
| la latitude | *lines of latitude* |
| la longitude | *lines of longitude* |

| | |
|---|---|
| le compas | *the compass* |
| la boussole } | |
| le nord | *north* |
| le sud | *south* |
| l'est (m.) | *east* |
| l'ouest (m.) | *west* |
| les continents (m.pl.) | *the continents* |
| l'Afrique (f.) | *Africa* |
| l'Australie (f.) | *Australia* |

| | |
|---|---|
| l'Eurasie (f.) | *Eurasia* |
| l'Amérique (f.) | *America* |
| l'Antarctique (m.) | *Antarctic* |

### Les autres territoires
### *Other land masses*

| | |
|---|---|
| l'Europe (f.) | *Europe* |
| l'Extrême-Orient (m.) | *Far East* |
| l'Inde (f.) | *India* |
| le Moyen-Orient (m.) | *Middle East* |
| l'Amérique du Nord (f.) | *North America* |
| l'Amérique du Sud (f.) | *South America* |

| | |
|---|---|
| les océans (m.pl.) | *oceans* |
| l'Atlantique (m.) | *Atlantic* |
| le Pacifique | *Pacific* |
| l'océan Indien (m.) | *Indian Ocean* |
| l'océan Arctique (m.) | *Arctic Ocean* |
| l'Antarctique (m.) | *Antarctic Ocean* |

# 17 Le vaste monde *The wider world*

## LES PAYS D'EUROPE ET DE L'UNION EUROPÉENNE
### THE COUNTRIES OF EUROPE AND THE EUROPEAN UNION

| Le pays *Country* | | La nationalité *Nationality* | |
|---|---|---|---|
| L'EUROPE (F.) | *EUROPE* | EUROPÉEN(NE) | *EUROPEAN* |
| la Grande-Bretagne | *Great Britain* | britannique | *British* |
| l'Angleterre (f.) | *England* | anglais(e) | *English* |
| le pays de Galles | *Wales* | gallois(e) | *Welsh* |
| l'Irlande du Nord (f.) | *Northern Ireland* | irlandais(e) | *Irish* |
| l'Écosse (f.) | *Scotland* | écossais(e) | *Scottish* |
| la Scandinavie | *Scandinavia* | scandinave | *Scandinavian* |
| le Danemark | *Denmark* | danois(e) | *Danish* |
| la Finlande | *Finland* | finlandais(e) | *Finnish* |
| la Suède | *Sweden* | suédois(e) | *Swedish* |
| la Norvège | *Norway* | norvégien(ne) | *Norwegian* |
| l'Europe de l'Ouest (f.) } l'Europe occidentale | *Western Europe* | de l'Europe occidentale | *Western European* |
| la Belgique | *Belgium* | belge | *Belgian* |
| la France | *France* | français(e) | *French* |
| l'Allemagne (f.) | *Germany* | allemand(e) | *German* |
| la Hollande | *Holland* | hollandais(e) | *Dutch* |
| la Hongrie | *Hungary* | hongrois(e) | *Hungarian* |
| l'Italie (f.) | *Italy* | italien(ne) | *Italian* |
| le Luxembourg | *Luxemburg* | luxembourgeois(e) | *from Luxembourg* |
| la Pologne | *Poland* | polonais(e) | *Polish* |
| le Portugal | *Portugal* | portugais(e) | *Portuguese* |
| l'Espagne (f.) | *Spain* | espagnol(e) | *Spanish* |
| la Suisse | *Switzerland* | suisse | *Swiss* |
| l'Europe Centrale (f.) | *Central Europe* | de l'Europe Centrale | *Central European* |
| l'Autriche (f.) | *Austria* | autrichien(ne) | *Austrian* |
| la Bosnie | *Bosnia* | bosniaque | *Bosnian* |
| la Bulgarie | *Bulgaria* | bulgare | *Bulgarian* |
| la Croatie | *Croatia* | croate | *Croatian* |
| la République Tchèque | *Czech Republic* | tchèque | *Czech* |

# 17 Le vaste monde *The wider world*

| la Grèce | *Greece* | grec(que) | *Greek* |
|---|---|---|---|
| la Roumanie | *Romania* | roumain(e) | *Romanian* |
| la Russie | *Russia* | russe | *Russian* |
| la Serbie | *Serbia* | serbe | *Serbian* |
| la Slovaquie | *Slovakia* | slovaque | *Slovak* |
| la Slovénie | *Slovenia* | slovène | *Slovenian* |
| la Turquie | *Turkey* | turc/turque | *Turkish* |

**AILLEURS**                 ***ELSEWHERE***

| l'Algérie (f.) | *Algeria* | algérien(ne) | *Algerian* |
|---|---|---|---|
| la Chine | *China* | chinois(e) | *Chinese* |
| l'Inde (f.) | *India* | indien(ne) | *Indian* |
| l'Irak (m.) | *Iraq* | irakien(ne) | *Iraqi* |
| l'Israël (m.) | *Israel* | israélien(ne) | *Israeli* |
| le Japon | *Japan* | japonais(e) | *Japanese* |
| le Maroc | *Morocco* | marocain(e) | *Moroccan* |
| la Tunisie | *Tunisia* | tunisien(ne) | *Tunisian* |
| les Etats-Unis (m. pl.) | *U.S.A.* | américain(e) | *American* |

Note: In general, for a language use the masculine form of the nationality.
e.g.      Elle est allemande. Elle parle allemand.
          Ils sont italiens. Ils parlent italien.

However, there are some exceptions.
e.g.      Il est algérien. Il parle arabe at français.
          Les Belges parlent français, flamand et wallon.

For an inhabitant of a country, use the nationality with an initial capital letter.
e.g.      Les Portugais et les Espagnols sont voisins.

## Les grandes villes *Important cities*

**En France:**

| | | | |
|---|---|---|---|
| Paris | Lyon | Marseille | Bordeaux |
| Lille | Rennes | Nice | Strasbourg |
| Clermont-Ferrand | | Brest | Nantes |
| Montpellier | | Toulouse | Grenoble |

**Ailleurs: Elsewhere:**

| | | | |
|---|---|---|---|
| Londres | *London* | Venise | *Venice* |
| Le Caire | *Cairo* | Moscou | *Moscow* |
| Vienne | *Vienna* | Bruxelles | *Brussels* |
| Genève | *Geneva* | Rome | *Rome* |
| Edimbourg | *Edinburgh* | Athènes | *Athens* |

## *ENCORE!*

● *Activity: Fill in the names of the countries at this meeting in Strasbourg.*

## LES ORGANISATIONS NATIONALES ET INTERNATIONALES
*NATIONAL AND INTERNATIONAL AGENCIES*

### Les organisations nationales *National organisations*

| | |
|---|---|
| l'Agence Nationale Pour l'Emploi (ANPE) | *Job Centre* |
| la Société Nationale des Chemins de fer Français (SNCF) | *French Railways* |
| la Société Protectrice des Animaux (SPA) | *Equivalent of RSPCA* |

### L'Union européenne *The European Union*

| | |
|---|---|
| le président | *the president* |
| le Conseil de l'Europe | *Council of Europe* |
| le/la député(e) européen(ne) | *Euro MP (MEP)* |

### Les organisations mondiales *World organisations*

| | |
|---|---|
| les Nations Unies | *United Nations* |
| l'Organisation Mondiale pour la Santé | *World Health Organisation* |
| la Croix Rouge | *Red Cross* |
| l'OTAN | *NATO* |
| Greenpeace | *Greenpeace* |

# 17 Le vaste monde *The wider world*

## NOUVELLES INTERNATIONALES
### *INTERNATIONAL NEWS ITEMS*

| | |
|---|---|
| les nouvelles les informations (f.pl.) | *news* |
| le désastre | *disaster* |
| l'accident (m.) | *accident* |
| l'avalanche (f.) | *avalanche* |
| l'explosion d'une bombe (f.) | *bomb explosion* |
| le cyclone | *cyclone* |
| la sécheresse | *drought* |
| le tremblement de terre | *earthquake* |
| l'incendie (f.) | *fire* |
| l'inondation (f). | *flood* |
| l'ouragan (m.) | *hurricane* |
| le glissement de terrain | *landslide* |
| la tempête | *storm, tempest* |
| le terrorisme | *terrorism* |
| la tornade | *tornado* |
| le typhon | *typhoon* |
| l'éruption (f.) volcanique | *volcanic eruption* |

| | |
|---|---|
| la catastrophe aérienne | *plane crash* |
| l'assassinat (m.) | *assassination* |
| l'attentat (m.) | *attack* |
| l'attentat à la bombe | *terrorist bombing* |
| l'assemblée (f.) la conférence le congrès | *conference* |
| le cessez-le-feu | *cease-fire* |
| la rencontre au sommet | *summit meeting* |
| la manifestation | *demonstration* |
| l'émeute (f.) | *riot* |
| blessé(e) | *wounded* |
| brûlé(e) | *burned* |
| en état de choc | *shocked* |
| l'explosion (f.) | *explosion* |
| la victime | *victim* |
| le survivant la survivante | *survivor* |
| écrire/rédiger | *to write* |
| imprimer | *to print* |
| mourir | *to die* |
| être tué(e) | *to be killed* |
| être blessé(e) | *to be injured* |

---

### *Typical newspaper quotations*

| | |
|---|---|
| Une bombe a explosé à ... | *Bomb blast in ...* |
| Des émeutes ont éclaté à ... | *Fighting has broken out ...* |
| De nouveaux efforts afin de ... | *New efforts to ...* |
| Les gouvernements cherchent un accord sur ... | *Governments seek agreement on...* |
| Tempête prévue ... | *Storms threaten ...* |
| Des inondations meurtrières ont tué ... | *Floods kill ...* |

# 17 **Le vaste monde** *The wider world*

## L'ESPACE
### *SPACE*

| | |
|---|---|
| l'astéroïde (m.) | *asteroid* |
| l'astronaute (m.) | *astronaut* |
| le trou noir | *black hole* |
| le cosmos | *cosmos* |
| la galaxie | *galaxy* |
| l'année lumière (f.) | *light year* |
| la météore | *meteor* |
| la météorite | *meteorite* |
| la Voie Lactée | *Milky Way* |
| la lune | *moon* |
| la nébuleuse | *nebula* |
| la couche d'ozone | *ozone layer* |
| la planète | *planet* |
| le satellite | *satellite* |
| la navette | *shuttle* |
| l'engin spatial (m.) | { *space craft* / *space ship* |
| la station de l'espace | *space station* |
| la vitesse de la lumière | *speed of light* |
| du son | *of sound* |
| l'étoile (f.) | *star* |
| le télescope | *telescope* |
| l'OVNI (objet volant non identifié) (m.) | *UFO* |
| l'univers (m.) | *universe* |
| la fusée | *rocket* |
| tourner autour de | *to circle* |
| orbiter autour de | *to orbit* |

## LES ABRÉVIATIONS
### *ABBREVIATIONS*

| | |
|---|---|
| M | *Mr* |
| MM | *Gentlemen* |
| Mmes | *Mrs / Ladies* |
| Mlle | *Ms / Miss* |
| Mgr | *Monseigneur* (title for cardinal) |
| Me (Maître) | *Title for lawyer* |
| | |
| Licencié ès Lettres | *B.A.* |
| Maîtrise ès Lettres | *M.A.* |
| Licencié ès Sciences | *B.Sc.* |
| ANPE (Agence nationale pour l'emploi) | *Job Centre* |
| HLM (habitation à loyer modéré) | *Council house / flat* |
| ENA (École Nationale d'Administration) | *One of the* Grandes Écoles *producing France's administrative elite* |
| PNB (Produit national brut) | *Gross National Product* |
| PC (Parti Communiste) | *Communist Party* |
| PS (Parti Socialiste) | *Socialist Party* |
| PTT (Postes, Télégraphes, Téléphones) | *Post Office* |
| PDG (Président-directeur général) | *Managing director* |
| PV (Procès Verbal) | *Booking, by policeman* |
| RF (République Française) | *French Republic* |
| RPR (Rassemblement pour la République) | *French political party (right-wing)* |
| RSVP (Répondez, s'il vous plaît) | *RSVP* |
| SIDA (Syndrome immuno-déficitaire acquis) | *AIDS* |
| SMIC (Salaire minimum interprofessionnel de croissance) | *Guaranteed minimum income* |
| TVA (Taxe à la valeur ajoutée) | *VAT* |
| UDF (Union pour la démocratie française) | *French political party (centre-right)* |

# 18 Coda *Extras*

## L'ARGOT ET LES JURONS
### *SLANG AND EXPLETIVES*

You are advised not to use this language yourself as it is likely to give offence, but you may find it useful to be able to understand it!

It is especially difficult for a non-native speaker to judge when slang can be used, how much offence it is likely to give and what reaction it is likely to bring on. Ask yourself how you would react to being sworn at by a foreigner, and try to find other ways of responding!

| | |
|---|---|
| Mince! Zut! | *Hell, Damn, Blast* |
| Putain! | *Bloody hell!* |
| Merde! | *Shit! Bugger!* |
| Casse-toi! Fous-moi la paix! | *Piss off!* |
| Va te faire foutre! | *F\*\*\* off!* |
| Laisse-moi tranquille! | *Leave me alone!* |
| Va te faire voir! | *Get lost! Get stuffed!* |
| Mais qu'est-ce que tu veux? | *What the hell do you want?* |
| | |
| Génial! / Super! | *Wow!* |
| Berk! | *Yuk!* |

You should also be aware of the various hand signs, most of which are quite offensive.

| | |
|---|---|
| le bouquin | *book* |
| le / la frangin (-e) | *brother / sister* |
| la bagnole | *car* ('wheels') |
| les flics (m. pl.) | *cops* |
| le clébard | *dog ('mutt')* |
| la nana la gonzesse | *girl* ('chick'); *woman* |
| le flingue | *gun* ('shooter') |
| la baraque | *house* |
| le pognon les sous (m. pl.) | *money* ('dough, lolly') |

| | |
|---|---|
| le boulot | *work, job* |
| les godasses (f. pl.) les pompes (f. pl) | *shoes* |
| les chiottes (f. pl.) | *toilets* |
| bouffer | *to eat* |
| avoir la gueule de bois | *to have a hangover* |
| bosser | *to work* |

# 18 Coda *Extras*

## EXCUSEZ-MOI, S'IL VOUS PLAÎT
### *EXCUSE ME, PLEASE*

| | |
|---|---|
| Au secours! | *Help!* |
| | |
| Parlez-vous anglais? | *Do you speak English?* |
| Excusez-moi! | *Sorry! Pardon me!* |
| Je suis désolé(e). | *I'm sorry.* |
| Pardon. | *Excuse me.* |
| Je ne comprends pas. | *I don't understand.* |
| Vous pouvez répéter, s'il vous plaît? | *Can you repeat that please?* |
| Plus lentement, s'il vous plaît. | *Can you say it more slowly?* |
| Comment? | *Pardon?* |
| Qu'est-ce que c'est en anglais? | *What does that mean in English?* |
| Vous parlez ...? | *Do you speak ...?* |
| Comment vous épelez / écrivez cela? | *How do you spell / write it?* |
| Vous pouvez écrire cela pour moi, s'il vous plaît? | *Can you write that down for me, please?* |
| Vous pouvez m'aider? | *Can you help me?* |
| Vous comprenez? | *Do you understand?* |
| | |
| S'il vous plaît. | *Please.* |
| Merci. | *Thank you.* |
| Il n'y a pas de quoi! | *Don't mention it.* |
| Écoutez! | *Listen!* |
| Je suis désolé, je ne voulais pas faire de mal. | *I'm sorry, I did not mean to give offence.* |
| Pardon, j'ai mal compris. | *Sorry, I misunderstood.* |
| Je crois que vous m'avez mal compris. | *I'm afraid you have misunderstood me.* |
| | |
| C'était de ma faute. | *It was my fault.* |
| Ce n'était pas de ma faute. | *It was NOT my fault.* |
| C'était de votre faute. | *It was your fault.* |
| | |
| Danger! | *Danger!* |
| Attention! | *Watch out!* |
| Sois / soyez prudent! | *Be careful!* |
| Dangereux! | *Dangerous!* |

# 18 Coda *Extras*

## LES SERVICES D'URGENCE
### *EMERGENCY SERVICES*

| | |
|---|---|
| Police | *Police* |
| Pompiers | *Fire brigade* |
| Hôpital | *Hospital* |
| Ambulance | *Ambulance* |
| Dépannage Auto | *Road assistance (AA)* |
| Renseignements | *Information* |

## EMERGENCY TELEPHONE NUMBERS

Police: 17
Fire brigade: 18
Hospital: 15
Directory inquiries: 12

These numbers can be called free of charge from any phone box, simply by dialling the two digits given.

# Key to the Activities

**Greetings** **1:** *Morning*: Bonjour!; *Day*: Bonjour!; *Evening*: Bonsoir!; *Night*: Bonne nuit!
**2:** Bonjour, Monsieur; Bonjour, mademoiselle; Bonjour, Madame
**Numbers:** **3:** Virginie est première; Marie est seconde; Paulette est troisième

**The Calendar** (b) le dix mai; le seize juillet; le vingt-deux octobre; le premier mars; le quinze décembre

**The Time** (a) une heure et quart (b) deux heures et demie (c) trois heures moins le quart (d) quatre heures (e) cinq heures moins le quart (f) treize heures cinq (g) quatorze heures vingt-cinq (h) seize heures cinquante (i) vingt-deux heures quarante-cinq (j) minuit moins une *or* vingt-trois heures cinquante-neuf

**Colours** **2:** (*UK*) bleu, blanc, rouge; (*Italy*) vert, blanc, rouge; (*France*) bleu, blanc, rouge; (*Germany*) rouge, jaune, noir; (*Spain*) rouge, jaune, rouge

**Where is it?** Il est (a) derrière le mur (b) sous la table (c) devant le cinéma (d) entre Pierre et Marie

**Questions** (*possible answers*) Quelle heure est-il?; C'est combien?; Qui c'est/qui est la?; C'est quelle marque de voiture?; Où se retrouve-t-on?; Pourquoi avez-vous du retard?

**Verbs** Hier il est parti à la pêche; aujourd'hui il joue au golf; demain il va faire du vélo. Hier elle a travaillé; ;aujourd'hui elle fait le ménage et la cuisine; demain elle va partir!

**Personal Matters** Elle adore cet homme; il est fana du football; elle déteste son gros ventre; elle admire cette fille.

**Birth, Marriage and Death** Maman a perdu . . . la couche; le hochet; le biberon; la tétine; la serviette; le bavoir; le bébé!

**Clothes and Fashion** Ils portent . . . un imperméable; un chapeau; des bottes . . . Ils ne portent rien du tout! Dans la valise ils mettent . . . un pull-over, une jupe, des gants, une chemise, des chaussettes, un tee-shirt, un pantalon, un pyjama Ils vont acheter . . . (a) une bague (b) des boucles d'oreilles (c) un collier (d) une bouteille de parfum (e) un atomiseur

**Food and Drink** Je voudrais . . . (a) deux verres de vin blanc et un verre de vin rouge (b) trois bières (c) un café noir et deux chocolats chauds, s'il vous plaît . . .

**Appointments** Excusez-moi, . . . (a) j'ai un rendez-vous chez le dentiste (b) j'ai raté le bus (c) ma voiture est tombée en panne (d) je vais jouer au golf (e) j'ai trop de travail (f) je vais manger au restaurant avec un(e) ami(e).

**The body and health** éponge; savon; déodorant; rasoir; peigne; shampooing

**Town and Shopping** Je les veux . . . (a) frisés (b) lavés (c) coupés (d) séchés

**The Natural World** le marais; l'arbre à feuilles caduques; le conifère, les montagnes; le château; l'étang; l'église